HOMESTEAD COOKBOOK

MEGA BUNDLE – 2 Manuscripts in 1 – 80+ Homestead friendly recipes including, roast, ice-cream, pie and casseroles for a delicious and tasty diet

TABLE OF CONTENTS

Introduction

Homestead recipes for personal enjoyment but also for family enjoyment. You will love them for sure for how easy it is to prepare them.

ROAST RECIPES

ROASTED TOMATO

Serves: **3-4**

Prep Time: **10** Minutes

Cook Time: **20** Minutes

Total Time: **30** Minutes

INGREDIENTS

- 1 lb. tomatoes
- 2 tablespoons olive oil
- 1 tsp curry powder
- 1 tsp salt

DIRECTIONS

1. Preheat the oven to 400 F
2. Cut everything in half lengthwise
3. Toss everything with olive oil and place onto a prepared baking sheet
4. Roast for 18-20 minutes at 400 F or until golden brown
5. When ready remove from the oven and serve

ROASTED SQUASH

Serves: **3-4**
Prep Time: **10**   Minutes

Cook Time: **20**   Minutes

Total Time: **30**   Minutes

INGREDIENTS

- 2 delicata squashes
- 2 tablespoons olive oil
- 1 tsp curry powder
- 1 tsp salt

DIRECTIONS

1. Preheat the oven to 400 F
2. Cut everything in half lengthwise
3. Toss everything with olive oil and place onto a prepared baking sheet
4. Roast for 18-20 minutes at 400 F or until golden brown
5. When ready remove from the oven and serve

ROASTED EGGPLANT

Serves: **4**

Prep Time: **10** Minutes

Cook Time: **45** Minutes

Total Time: **55** Minutes

INGREDIENTS

- 2 eggplants
- 1 tablespoon olive oil
- 5 olives
- 2 cups canned cannellini
- 1 anchovy fillets
- 1 tablespoon lemon juice
- 1 tsp salt
- 1 cloves garlic
- ¼ chopped fresh parsley
- 2 dried tomatoes

DIRECTIONS

1. Roast the eggplant in oven at 375 F for 40 minutes
2. In a blender add garlic and eggplant and add olive oil, parsley, tomato, beans, olives and lemon juice

Blend mixture until smooth remove and serve

SOUP RECIPES

ZUCCHINI SOUP

Serves: **4**

Prep Time: **10**   Minutes

Cook Time: **20**   Minutes

Total Time: **30**   Minutes

INGREDIENTS

- 1 tablespoon olive oil
- 1 lb. zucchini
- ¼ red onion
- ½ cup all-purpose flour
- ¼ tsp salt
- ¼ tsp pepper
- 1 can vegetable broth
- 1 cup heavy cream

DIRECTIONS

1. In a saucepan heat olive oil and sauté zucchini until tender
2. Add remaining ingredients to the saucepan and bring to a boil
3. When all the vegetables are tender transfer to a blender and blend until smooth
4. Pour soup into bowls, garnish with parsley and serve

CHIPOTLE BEAN SOUP

Serves: **2**
Prep Time: **10**   Minutes

Cook Time: **20**   Minutes

Total Time: **30**   Minutes

INGREDIENTS

- ½ small onion
- 2 tsp olive oil
- 1 clove garlic
- 2 cups chicken broth
- ¼ chipotle chili powder
- baby carrots

DIRECTIONS

1. In a saucepan sauce onion with olive oil for 2-3 minutes over medium heat
2. Add beans, garlic, chili powder and vegetable broth
3. Add baby carrots and simmer for 12-15 minutes
4. Pure the mixture and season with salt

SIDE DISHES

SPINACH SPREAD

Serves: **4**

Prep Time: **10** Minutes

Cook Time: **20** Minutes

Total Time: **30** Minutes

INGREDIENTS

- 2 tsp canola oil
- ½ tsp lemon zest
- ½ tsp pepper
- ¼ grated nutmeg
- ½ cup water
- 2 10-ounce packages frozen spinach
- 1-ounce parmesan cheese
- 1 cup cottage cheese
- 2 tablespoons lemon juice
- 1 cup onion
- 2 cloves garlic

DIRECTIONS

1. In a skillet heat oil over medium heat and add garlic and onion
2. Cook for 7-8 minutes an add water and spinach

3. Transfer mixture in a blender and add parmesan cheese, lemon juice, cottage cheese, pepper, lemon zest, nutmeg, salt and puree until smooth

4. Refrigerate at least 4h before serving

LENTIL HUMMUS

Serves: **6**

Prep Time: **10** Minutes

Cook Time: **30** Minutes

Total Time: **40** Minutes

INGREDIENTS

- 1 15-ounce can lentils
- ¼ tsp salt
- ¼ ground cumin
- ¼ cup water
- ½ cup sesame tahini
- 1 clove garlic
- ¼ cup olive oil
- 2 tablespoons lemon juice

DIRECTIONS

1. Mix all the ingredients except water in a blender and blend until smooth
2. Remove and serve

CUMIN SCENTED BEAN DIP

Serves: *4*
Prep Time: *10* Minutes

Cook Time: *10* Minutes

Total Time: *20* Minutes

INGREDIENTS

- 2 tablespoons olive oil
- ½ cup plain yogurt
- ½ tsp cumin
- ¼ tsp garlic
- pepper
- salt
- white beans

DIRECTIONS

1. In a blender add olive oil, white beans, cumin, yogurt, garlic and blend until smooth
2. Season with pepper or salt and serve with cucumber slices or pita

BEAN AND CORN TACOS

Serves: **2**

Prep Time: **10** Minutes

Cook Time: **20** Minutes

Total Time: **30** Minutes

INGREDIENTS

- Beans
- ½ cup corn salsa
- baby spinach
- ½ avocado

DIRECTIONS

1. In a saucepan mix beans with salsa
2. Simmer for 12-15 minutes and serve with tortillas and a pinch of cheese

BLACK BEAN SALAD WITH QUINOA

Serves: *2*
Prep Time: *10* Minutes

Cook Time: *20* Minutes

Total Time: *30* Minutes

INGREDIENTS

- ¼ cup dried quino
- 1 cup butternut squash
- 2 tablespoons water
- ¼ crumbled feta cheese
- 2 tablespoons cilantro
- salt

DIRECTIONS

1. In a saucepan add quinoa, squash and water and simmer for 12-15 minutes until squash is cooked
2. Stir in beans and feta cheese and cilantro
3. Remove from heat and season with salt

CREAMY SCRAMBLED EGGS

Serves: *2*
Prep Time: *10* Minutes

Cook Time: *30* Minutes

Total Time: *40* Minutes

INGREDIENTS

- 2 tablespoons milk
- salt
- 3 eggs
- 1/3 cup low fat cheese

DIRECTIONS

1. Beat the eggs with milk and salt
2. Cook in a nonstick pan over medium heat
3. Stir in cottage cheese remove and serve

CHICKEN CURRY WITH BROWN RICE

Serves: **2**
Prep Time: **10** Minutes

Cook Time: **20** Minutes

Total Time: **30** Minutes

INGREDIENTS

- 1 cup brown rice
- coconut milk
- 1 tsp curry paste
- vegetable mix

DIRECTIONS

1. In a saucepan simmer sliced vegetables in coconut milk and chicken and add Thai curry paste
2. Remove and serve over brown rice

Serves: **2**
Prep Time: **10**   Minutes

Cook Time: **20**   Minutes

Total Time: **30**   Minutes

INGREDIENTS

- Brown rice
- Black beans
- 1 avocado
- 1 cup lettuce
- 1 cup shredded cheese

DIRECTIONS

1. **Top brown rice with avocado, lettuce, beans and shredded cheese and serve**

LEMON ROSEMARY CHICKEN

Serves:	**4**
Prep Time:	**10** Minutes
Cook Time:	**30** Minutes
Total Time:	**40** Minutes

INGREDIENTS

- 4 6oz. boneless chicken breast
- 2 tsp olive oil
- 1 tsp lemon pepper seasoning
- 1 tsp salt
- 2 lemons
- fresh rosemary
- 1 cup chicken broth
- ½ tsp garlic

DIRECTIONS

1. Preheat oven to 350 F
2. Brush chicken with olive oil and sprinkle with lemon seasoning
3. In a baking dish place chicken with rosemary and top with lemon slices
4. Bake for 20-25 minutes or until golden brown
5. In a saucepan mix rosemary with chicken broth and garlic
6. Serve mixture with chicken and garnish with lemon slice

PAN CON TOMATE

Serves: **4**

Prep Time: **10** Minutes

Cook Time: **10** Minutes

Total Time: **20** Minutes

INGREDIENTS

- 1 baguette
- 2 beefsteak tomatoes
- 1 clove garlic
- ¼ olive oil

DIRECTIONS

1. Toast the bread and cut the garlic clove
2. Rub with ½ half cut tomato to cover
3. Drizzle with oil and sprinkle with salt

GREEN PESTO PASTA

Serves: *2*
Prep Time: *5*   Minutes
Cook Time: *15*   Minutes
Total Time: *20*   Minutes

INGREDIENTS

- 4 oz. spaghetti
- 2 cups basil leaves
- 2 garlic cloves
- ¼ cup olive oil
- 2 tablespoons parmesan cheese
- ½ tsp black pepper

DIRECTIONS

1. Bring water to a boil and add pasta
2. In a blend add parmesan cheese, basil leaves, garlic and blend
3. Add olive oil, pepper and blend again
4. Pour pesto onto pasta and serve when ready

Serves: **4**

Prep Time: **10**   Minutes

Cook Time: **30**   Minutes

Total Time: **40**   Minutes

INGREDIENTS

- 2 lb. asparagus spears
- 2 tablespoons fresh ginger
- 2 tablespoon quince jam
- 2 tablespoons olive oil
- 1 tsp lemon juice
- 2 tablespoons walnuts
- salt

DIRECTIONS

1. In a steamer add asparagus and steam until tender for 4-5 minutes
2. In a bowl whisk together, ginger, quince jam, olive oil, salt and lemon juice
3. Pour mixture over asparagus and sprinkle with walnuts

RISOTTO WITH MUSHROOMS

Serves: *2*
Prep Time: *10* Minutes

Cook Time: *30* Minutes

Total Time: *40* Minutes

INGREDIENTS

- 2/4 lb mushrooms
- ¼ parmesan cheese
- salt
- arugula
- ¼ lb zucchini
- 3 tablespoons olive oil
- ¼ cup white wine
- 1 onion
- 1 cup brown rice
- 3 cups chicken broth
- 2 tablespoons parsley
- 1 garlic clover

DIRECTIONS

1. In a saucepan heat olive oil and add zucchini, mushrooms and season with salt
2. Cook for 2-3 minutes and transfer to a plate

3. Add onion, rice and wine and cook for 4-5 minutes
4. Add broth and mushrooms, garlic, zucchini and parsley
5. Transfer to a place and garnish with parmesan and arugula

GRASSFED BEEF & QUINOA CHILI

Serves: **6**

Prep Time: **10**   Minutes

Cook Time: **30**   Minutes

Total Time: **40**   Minutes

INGREDIENTS

- 1 onion
- 2 cloves garlic
- 1 lb. ground grassfed beef
- 1 tsp salt
- 1 tablespoon chili powder
- 1 tablespoon cumin
- 1 can diced tomatoes
- 1 can tomato sauce
- 1 cup water
- 2 cans kidney beans

DIRECTIONS

1. In a pot sauté onion and garlic until soft
2. Add spices, beef and chili powder
3. Stir in tomato sauce, tomatoes, beans and simmer for 15-20 minutes
4. When thickens remove from heat and serve with guacamole

TOMATO BASIL ORZO

Serves: **4**

Prep Time: **5**   Minutes

Cook Time: **15**   Minutes

Total Time: **20**   Minutes

INGREDIENTS

- 1 cup orzo pasta
- ¼ cup basil leaves
- ¼ cup sun-dried tomatoes
- 1 tablespoon olive oil
- ¼ cup parmesan cheese
- ¼ tsp salt
- ¼ tsp black pepper

DIRECTIONS

1. In a pot bring water to a boil, add orzo and cook for 10 minutes
2. In a blender add basil leaves, sun-dried tomatoes and blend until smooth
3. In a bowl toss together the orzo, and basil mixture with olive oil and parmesan cheese
4. Serve when ready

AVOCADO WRAPS

Serves: **2**
Prep Time: **10** Minutes

Cook Time: **20** Minutes

Total Time: **30** Minutes

INGREDIENTS

- 1 lb. pack chicken pieces
- ¼ tsp chili powder
- 1 garlic clove
- 1 tsp olive oil
- 2 wraps
- 1 avocado
- 1 roasted red pepper

DIRECTIONS

1. In a bowl combine chicken, chili powder, lime juice and garlic
2. In a pan heat oil and fry the chicken mixture
3. Add mixture to each wrap and top with avocado and red pepper

Serves: **4**

Prep Time: **10** Minutes

Cook Time: **20** Minutes

Total Time: **30** Minutes

INGREDIENTS

- 100g penne
- 1 tsp olive oil
- 1 onion
- 1 pepper
- 1 garlic clove
- 1 tsp chili powder
- 1 tsp coriander
- ¼ tsp cumin seeds
- 1 lb. tomatoes
- 1 can sweetcorn
- 1 avocado
- ¼ lime

DIRECTIONS

1. Cook the pasta for 10-15 minutes
2. In a pan heat oil and sautéed onion, garlic and tomatoes
3. Stir in water, corn and simmer for another 12-15 minutes

4. Toss the avocado with lime juice
5. Place the pasta in the pot, add remaining ingredients, cook for another 2-3 minutes
6. When ready remove from heat and serve

TUNA LETTUCE WRAPS

Serves: **2**

Prep Time: **10** Minutes

Cook Time: **15** Minutes

Total Time: **25** Minutes

INGREDIENTS

- 2 tuna fillets
- 1 avocado
- 1 tsp mustard powder
- 1 tsp apple cider vinegar
- 6 romaine lettuce leaves
- 8-10 cherry tomatoes

DIRECTIONS

1. In a pan add tuna and cook for 1-2 minutes per side
2. Combine avocado with vinegar, mustard powder and mix well
3. Spoon avocado mixture into lettuce leaves and top with tomatoes
4. When ready serve with tuna

Serves: **2**
Prep Time: **5**   Minutes
Cook Time: **25** Minutes
Total Time: **35** Minutes

INGREDIENTS

- ¼ cup toovar
- ¼ cup moong dal
- ¼ cup chana dal
- 1 cup fenugreek
- 1 cup coriander
- ½ cup green peas
- ½ cup coconut
- 2 green chillies
- ¼ cup onions
- ¼ cup carrot
- salt

DIRECTIONS

1. Soak the dals in water for 2-3 hours
2. Grind dals to paste, add the rest of the ingredients and mix well
3. Steam the paste for 12-15 minutes or until everything is tender

4. When ready remove from heat and serve

CUCUMBER CHANA DAL

Serves: 2
Prep Time: 5 Minutes
Cook Time: 20 Minutes
Total Time: 25 Minutes

INGREDIENTS

- ½ cup cucumber
- ½ cup chana dal
- 1 tsp cumin seeds
- ½ tsp chili powder
- 1 tsp turmeric powder
- 1 tsp olive oil

DIRECTIONS

1. Soak the chana dal in water for 1-2 hours
2. In a pan add cumin seeds and sauté for 1-2 minutes
3. Add the rest of the ingredients in the pan and cook for 12-15 minutes
4. When ready remove from heat and serve

OATS AND BROWN RICE

Serves: **4**

Prep Time: **10** Minutes

Cook Time: **30** Minutes

Total Time: **40** Minutes

INGREDIENTS

- ¼ cup oats
- ½ cup cooked brown rice
- 1 tablespoon moong dal
- 1 tsp olive oil
- ¼ cup onions
- 1 tsp garlic
- ¼ tsp ginger
- ½ cup beans
- ¼ cup carrot
- ¼ cup green peas
- 1 tablespoon coriander

DIRECTIONS

1. In a pressure cooker add onions, garlic, ginger and sauté for 2-3 minutes
2. Add green peas, beans, carrot and sauté for another 2-3 minutes

36

3. Add the rest of the ingredients, water and cook for another 5-6 minutes
4. Cook until the water has evaporated
5. When ready remove from heat and serve

AVOCADO DIP

Serves: *1*

Prep Time: 5   Minutes

Cook Time: 5   Minutes

Total Time: *10*   Minutes

INGREDIENTS

- 1 cup avocado
- 1 tsp lemon juice
- 1 tablespoon tomatoes
- ¼ tsp green chillies
- salt

DIRECTIONS

1. In a blender combine all ingredients together
2. Blend until smooth
3. When ready remove and serve

BUCKWHEAT AND SPROUTS

Serves: **2**

Prep Time: **5** Minutes

Cook Time: **20** Minutes

Total Time: **25** Minutes

INGREDIENTS

- ½ cup buckwheat
- ½ cup sprouts
- ½ cup moong dal
- 1 tsp olive oil
- 1 black peppercorn
- ¼ tsp cumin seeds
- 2 cloves
- ¼ tsp turmeric powder

DIRECTIONS

1. In a pressure cooker add cloves, cumin seeds and peppercorn, sauté for 2-3 minutes
2. Add the rest of the ingredients and water
3. Simmer for 12-15 minutes or until vegetables are soft
4. When ready remove from heat and serve

Serves: *4*

Prep Time: *10* Minutes

Cook Time: *40* Minutes

Total Time: *50* Minutes

INGREDIENTS

- 1 cup brown rice
- Salt
- 1 tsp olive oil

DIRECTIONS

1. Soak the brown rice in water for 30-40 minutes
2. When ready transfer to a pressure cooker
3. Cook for 6 whistles, when ready remove and serve

BROCCOLI SALAD

Serves: **2**

Prep Time: **5** Minutes

Cook Time: **5** Minutes

Total Time: **10** Minutes

INGREDIENTS

- 1 cup broccoli
- 1 cup quinoa
- 2 radishes
- 2 tablespoons pumpkin seeds
- 1 cup salad dressing

DIRECTIONS

1. In a bowl combine all ingredients together and mix well
2. Serve with dressing

GREEK SALAD

Serves: 2
Prep Time: 5   Minutes

Cook Time: 5   Minutes

Total Time: 10   Minutes

INGREDIENTS

- 1 cup cherry tomatoes
- 1 cucumber
- 1 cup olives
- ½ cup onion
- 1 cup feta
- 1 cup salad dressing

DIRECTIONS

1. In a bowl combine all ingredients together and mix well
2. Serve with dressing

POTATO SALAD

Serves: *2*
Prep Time: *5*   Minutes

Cook Time: *5*   Minutes

Total Time: *10* Minutes

INGREDIENTS

- 1 lb. white potatoes
- 4 slices bacon
- ½ red onion
- ¼ cup apple cider vinegar
- 1 tablespoon olive oil
- 4 green onions
- 1 tablespoon mustard

DIRECTIONS

1. In a bowl combine all ingredients together and mix well
2. Serve with dressing

Serves: **2**

Prep Time: **5** Minutes

Cook Time: **5** Minutes

Total Time: **10** Minutes

INGREDIENTS

- ¼ cup olive oil
- Juice of ½ lemon
- 2 avocados
- 1 cup cherry tomatoes
- ½ cup corn
- 1 tablespoon cilantro

DIRECTIONS

1. In a bowl combine all ingredients together and mix well
2. Serve with dressing

Serves: **2**

Prep Time: **5**   Minutes

Cook Time: **5**   Minutes

Total Time: **10**   Minutes

INGREDIENTS

- ¼ cup olive oi
- 1 tablespoon apple cider vinegar
- 2 cups watermelon
- 1 cup cucumber
- 1 cup feta
- ¼ cup red onion
- ¼ cup mint

DIRECTIONS

1. In a bowl combine all ingredients together and mix well
2. Serve with dressing

Serves: 2

Prep Time: 5   Minutes

Cook Time: 5   Minutes

Total Time: *10*   Minutes

INGREDIENTS

- 2 cups corn
- 5 slices bacon
- 1 tablespoon cilantro
- 1 jalapeno
- ¼ cup mayonnaise
- 1 tsp chili powder
- 1 tsp garlic powder

DIRECTIONS

1. In a bowl combine all ingredients together and mix well
2. Serve with dressing

FISH STEW

Serves: **4**

Prep Time: **15**   Minutes

Cook Time: **45**   Minutes

Total Time: **60**   Minutes

INGREDIENTS

- 1 fennel bulb
- 1 red onion
- 2 garlic cloves
- 2 tablespoons olive oil
- 1 cup white wine
- 1 tablespoon fennel seeds
- 4 bay leaves
- 2 cups chicken stock
- 8 oz. halibut
- 12 oz. haddock

DIRECTIONS

1. Chop all ingredients in big chunks
2. In a large pot heat olive oil and add ingredients one by one
3. Cook for 5-6 or until slightly brown

4. Add remaining ingredients and cook until tender, 35-45 minutes
5. Season while stirring on low heat
6. When ready remove from heat and serve

BUTTERNUT SQUASH STEW

Serves: **4**

Prep Time: **15** Minutes

Cook Time: **45** Minutes

Total Time: **60** Minutes

INGREDIENTS

- 2 tablespoons olive oil
- 2 red onions
- 2 cloves garlic
- 1. Tablespoon rosemary
- 1 tablespoon thyme
- 2 lb. beef
- 1 cup white wine
- 1 cup butternut squash
- 2 cups beef broth
- ½ cup tomatoes
-

DIRECTIONS

1. Chop all ingredients in big chunks
2. In a large pot heat olive oil and add ingredients one by one
3. Cook for 5-6 or until slightly brown
4. Add remaining ingredients and cook until tender, 35-45 minutes

5. Season while stirring on low heat
6. When ready remove from heat and serve

ENCHILADA CASSEROLE

Serves: **4**

Prep Time: **10** Minutes

Cook Time: **25** Minutes

Total Time: **35** Minutes

INGREDIENTS

- 1 tablespoon olive oil
- 1 red onion
- 1 bell pepper
- 2 cloves garlic
- 1 can black beans
- 1 cup chicken
- 1 can green chilis
- 1 can enchilada sauce
- 1 cup cheddar cheese
- 1 cup sour cream

DIRECTIONS

1. Sauté the veggies and set aside
2. Preheat the oven to 425 F

3. Transfer the sautéed veggies to a baking dish, add remaining ingredients to the baking dish

4. Mix well, add seasoning and place the dish in the oven

5. Bake for 15-25 minutes or until slightly brown

6. When ready remove from the oven and serve

CHICKEN CASSEROLE

Serves: *4*
Prep Time: *10* Minutes

Cook Time: *15* Minutes

Total Time: *25* Minutes

INGREDIENTS

- 1 tablespoon olive oil
- 1 lb. chicken breast
- 1 red onion
- 2 cloves garlic
- 1 tsp paprika
- 4 cups cooked rice
- ¼ cup cranberries
- 1 lb. brussels sprouts
- 1 potato

DIRECTIONS

1. Sauté the veggies and set aside
2. Preheat the oven to 425 F
3. Transfer the sautéed veggies to a baking dish, add remaining ingredients to the baking dish
4. Mix well, add seasoning and place the dish in the oven
5. Bake for 12-15 minutes or until slightly brown

6. When ready remove from the oven and serve

CASSEROLE PIZZA

Serves: **6-8**
Prep Time: **10**   Minutes

Cook Time: **15**   Minutes

Total Time: **25**   Minutes

INGREDIENTS

- 1 pizza crust
- ½ cup tomato sauce
- ¼ black pepper
- 1 cup zucchini slices
- 1 cup mozzarella cheese
- 1 cup olives

DIRECTIONS

1. Spread tomato sauce on the pizza crust
2. Place all the toppings on the pizza crust
3. Bake the pizza at 425 F for 12-15 minutes
4. When ready remove pizza from the oven and serve

SECOND COOKBOOK

BREAKFAST RECIPES

ZUCCHINI APPLE PANCAKES

Serves: **4**

Prep Time: **10**   minutes

Cook Time: **10**   minutes

Total Time: **20**   minutes

INGREDIENTS

- 1 zucchini
- 2 tablespoons almond butter
- 2 eggs
- 1 tablespoon honey
- 2 tablespoons coconut oil
- 1 apple
- 1 cup almond flour
- ¼ tsp baking powder
- ¼ tsp sea salt

DIRECTIONS

1. Mix zucchini, honey, apples, thyme and almond butter in a bowl
2. In another bowl mix salt, baking powder and flour and beat the eggs
3. Mix all the ingredients from the bowl and heat coconut oil in a fry pan

4. Pour the mixture in the pan and cook for 1-2 minutes each side

QUINOA AND GOJI BERRIES

Serves: **4**

Prep Time: **5**   Minutes

Cook Time: **10** Minutes

Total Time: **15** Minutes

INGREDIENTS

- 1 cup quinoa
- 1 cup goji
- parsley as needed

DIRECTIONS

1. Soak the quinoa and goji grains for 5-6 minutes in water
2. Cook quinoa until soft for 10-15 minutes
3. Roast the cumin seeds in a hot pan and stir in goji berries and sprinkle with parsley

Serves: **2**

Prep Time: **10**   Minutes

Cook Time: **20**   Minutes

Total Time: **30**   Minutes

INGREDIENTS

- 2 cloves garlic
- 2 sausages
- ¼ onion
- ¼ cup carrot
- 2 cups mushrooms
- 1 tsp coconut oil
- ¼ tablespoon parsley
- 2 cups asparagus

DIRECTIONS

1. Sauté the garlic and onions in coconut oil and add the rest of the ingredients
2. Add the sausages and cook for 5-10 minutes, serve when ready

Serves: *3*

Prep Time: *10*   Minutes

Cook Time: *10*   Minutes

Total Time: *20*   Minutes

INGREDIENTS

- 1 cauliflower heat
- 1 tablespoon salt
- 1 tablespoon pepper
- - basil
- 1 tablespoon coconut oil
- 1 tablespoon parsley

DIRECTIONS

1. Grate the cauliflower to rice-grain
2. In a pan melt coconut oil add basil and add cauliflower and cook for 5-10 minutes
3. Cook until ready, remove and serve

HOMEMADE GRANOLA

Serves: **2**
Prep Time: **10** Minutes

Cook Time: **10** Minutes

Total Time: **20** Minutes

INGREDIENTS

- ¼ cup pumpkin seeds
- ¼ cup apricots
- 1 cup pecans
- ¼ cup almonds
- 1 cup coconut
- ½ cup coconut oil
- ½ cup honey
- 1 tsp cinnamon
- ¼ tsp nutmeg

DIRECTIONS

1. Preheat the oven to 325 F
2. Combine all the ingredients and toss well
3. Spread the mixture on a baking sheet (grease it with coconut oil) and bake for 10-15 minutes
4. When ready remove from oven and stir apricots
5. Let it cool and serve

Serves: *2*
Prep Time: *10* Minutes

Cook Time: *10* Minutes

Total Time: *20* Minutes

INGREDIENTS

- 2 eggs
- zest of ½ orange
- butter
- 2 tablespoons milk
- 10 slices fruit bread

DIRECTIONS

1. In a bowl mix eggs, orange zest and eggs, beat the eggs before and mix everything together
2. Place a slice of bread into the mixture to soak
3. Place a pan over medium heat
4. Place the bread slices in the pan and cook for 1-2 minutes on each side
5. Remove and serve with maple syrup

COCONUT OMELETTE

Serves: **4**

Prep Time: **10**   Minutes

Cook Time: **10**   Minutes

Total Time: **20**   Minutes

INGREDIENTS

- 2 eggs
- ½ tsp honey
- 1 tsp coconut oil

DIRECTIONS

1. In a bowl beat 2 eggs, add honey and stir
2. In a frying pan heat coconut oil over medium heat and pour the mixture
3. Cook on each side for 1-2 minutes
4. Remove and serve with salt or pepper

BANANA BREAKFAST CHEESECAKE

Serves: *1*
Prep Time: *10* Minutes

Cook Time: *10* Minutes

Total Time: *20* Minutes

INGREDIENTS

-   2 tsp chocolate chips
-   vanilla extract
-   1 tsp almond butter
-   1 tsp honey
-   2 tablespoons oats
-   1 tablespoon cream cheese
-   1 banana

DIRECTIONS

1. In a bowl mix almond butter, oats and honey
2. Slice a banana and add it to the mixture
3. In the microwave add chocolate chips for 1 minute, add vanilla extract and cream cheese to the melted chocolate
4. Top the banana with chocolate mixture and serve

Serves: **4**

Prep Time: **10**   Minutes

Cook Time: **30**   Minutes

Total Time: **40**   Minutes

INGREDIENTS

- 1 cup whole wheat flour
- ¼ tsp baking soda
- ¼ tsp baking powder
- 2 tablespoons goji berries
- 2 eggs
- 1 cup milk

DIRECTIONS

1. In a bowl combine all ingredients together and mix well
2. In a skillet heat olive oil
3. Pour ¼ of the batter and cook each pancake for 1-2 minutes per side
4. When ready remove from heat and serve

KIWI PANCAKES

Serves: **4**

Prep Time: **10** Minutes

Cook Time: **20** Minutes

Total Time: **30** Minutes

INGREDIENTS

- 1 cup whole wheat flour
- ¼ tsp baking soda
- ¼ tsp baking powder
- 1 cup mashed kiwi
- 2 eggs
- 1 cup milk

DIRECTIONS

1. In a bowl combine all ingredients together and mix well
2. In a skillet heat olive oil
3. Pour ¼ of the batter and cook each pancake for 1-2 minutes per side
4. When ready remove from heat and serve

MANGO PANCAKES

Serves: *4*

Prep Time: *10*   Minutes

Cook Time: *20*   Minutes

Total Time: *30*   Minutes

INGREDIENTS

- 1 cup whole wheat flour
- ¼ tsp baking soda
- ¼ tsp baking powder
- 1 cup mashed mango
- 2 eggs
- 1 cup milk

DIRECTIONS

1. In a bowl combine all ingredients together and mix well
2. In a skillet heat olive oil
3. Pour ¼ of the batter and cook each pancake for 1-2 minutes per side
4. When ready remove from heat and serve

SIMPLE PANCAKES

Serves: **4**

Prep Time: **10**   Minutes

Cook Time: **30**   Minutes

Total Time: **40**   Minutes

INGREDIENTS

- 1 cup whole wheat flour
- ¼ tsp baking soda
- ¼ tsp baking powder
- 2 eggs
- 1 cup milk

DIRECTIONS

1. In a bowl combine all ingredients together and mix well
2. In a skillet heat olive oil
3. Pour ¼ of the batter and cook each pancake for 1-2 minutes per side
4. When ready remove from heat and serve

GINGERBREAD MUFFINS

Serves: *8-12*

Prep Time: *10*   Minutes

Cook Time: *20*   Minutes

Total Time: *30*   Minutes

INGREDIENTS

- 2 eggs
- 1 tablespoon olive oil
- 1 cup milk
- 2 cups whole wheat flour
- 1 tsp baking soda
- ¼ tsp baking soda
- 1 tsp ginger
- 1 tsp cinnamon
- ¼ cup molasses

DIRECTIONS

1. In a bowl combine all dry ingredients
2. In another bowl combine all dry ingredients
3. Combine wet and dry ingredients together
4. Fold in ginger and mix well
5. Pour mixture into 8-12 prepared muffin cups, fill 2/3 of the cups

6. Bake for 18-20 minutes at 375 F

7. When ready remove from the oven and serve

PEAR MUFFINS

Serves: *8-12*
Prep Time: *10*   Minutes

Cook Time: *20*   Minutes

Total Time: *30*   Minutes

INGREDIENTS

- 2 eggs
- 1 tablespoon olive oil
- 1 cup milk
- 2 cups whole wheat flour
- 1 tsp baking soda
- ¼ tsp baking soda
- 1 tsp cinnamon
- 1 cup mashed pear

DIRECTIONS

1. In a bowl combine all dry ingredients
2. In another bowl combine all dry ingredients
3. Combine wet and dry ingredients together
4. Pour mixture into 8-12 prepared muffin cups, fill 2/3 of the cups
5. Bake for 18-20 minutes at 375 F
6. When ready remove from the oven and serve

POMELO MUFFINS

Serves: **8-12**
Prep Time: **10** Minutes

Cook Time: **20** Minutes

Total Time: **30** Minutes

INGREDIENTS

- 2 eggs
- 1 tablespoon olive oil
- 1 cup milk
- 2 cups whole wheat flour
- 1 tsp baking soda
- ¼ tsp baking soda
- 1 tsp cinnamon
- 1 cup pomelo

DIRECTIONS

1. In a bowl combine all dry ingredients
2. In another bowl combine all dry ingredients
3. Combine wet and dry ingredients together
4. Pour mixture into 8-12 prepared muffin cups, fill 2/3 of the cups
5. Bake for 18-20 minutes at 375 F
6. When ready remove from the oven and serve

APPLE MUFFINS

Serves: **8-12**

Prep Time: **10** Minutes

Cook Time: **20** Minutes

Total Time: **30** Minutes

INGREDIENTS

- 2 eggs
- 1 tablespoon olive oil
- 1 cup milk
- 2 cups whole wheat flour
- 1 tsp baking soda
- ¼ tsp baking soda
- 1 tsp cinnamon
- 1 cup apple

DIRECTIONS

1. In a bowl combine all dry ingredients
2. In another bowl combine all dry ingredients
3. Combine wet and dry ingredients together
4. Pour mixture into 8-12 prepared muffin cups, fill 2/3 of the cups
5. Bake for 18-20 minutes at 375 F
6. When ready remove from the oven and serve

CHOCOLATE MUFFINS

Serves: *8-12*
Prep Time: *10*   Minutes

Cook Time: *20*   Minutes

Total Time: *30*   Minutes

INGREDIENTS

- 2 eggs
- 1 tablespoon olive oil
- 1 cup milk
- 2 cups whole wheat flour
- 1 tsp baking soda
- ¼ tsp baking soda
- 1 tsp cinnamon
- 1 cup chocolate chips

DIRECTIONS

1. In a bowl combine all dry ingredients
2. In another bowl combine all dry ingredients
3. Combine wet and dry ingredients together
4. Fold in chocolate chips and mix well
5. Pour mixture into 8-12 prepared muffin cups, fill 2/3 of the cups
6. Bake for 18-20 minutes at 375 F

7. When ready remove from the oven and serve

SIMPLE MUFFINS

Serves: *8-12*
Prep Time: *10*   Minutes
Cook Time: *20*   Minutes
Total Time: *30*   Minutes

INGREDIENTS

- 2 eggs
- 1 tablespoon olive oil
- 1 cup milk
- 2 cups whole wheat flour
- 1 tsp baking soda
- ¼ tsp baking soda
- 1 tsp cinnamon

DIRECTIONS

1. In a bowl combine all dry ingredients
2. In another bowl combine all dry ingredients
3. Combine wet and dry ingredients together
4. Pour mixture into 8-12 prepared muffin cups, fill 2/3 of the cups
5. Bake for 18-20 minutes at 375 F
6. When ready remove from the oven and serve

SPINACH OMELETTE

Serves: *1*
Prep Time: *5*   Minutes
Cook Time: *10* Minutes
Total Time: *15* Minutes

INGREDIENTS

- 2 eggs
- ¼ tsp salt
- ¼ tsp black pepper
- 1 tablespoon olive oil
- ¼ cup cheese
- ¼ tsp basil
- 1 cup spinach

DIRECTIONS

1. In a bowl combine all ingredients together and mix well
2. In a skillet heat olive oil and pour the egg mixture
3. Cook for 1-2 minutes per side
4. When ready remove omelette from the skillet and serve

CUCUMBER OMELETTE

Serves: *1*
Prep Time: *5*   Minutes

Cook Time: *10*   Minutes

Total Time: *15*   Minutes

INGREDIENTS

- 2 eggs
- ¼ tsp salt
- ¼ tsp black pepper
- 1 tablespoon olive oil
- ¼ cup cheese
- ¼ tsp basil
- ½ cup cucumber

DIRECTIONS

1. In a bowl combine all ingredients together and mix well
2. In a skillet heat olive oil and pour the egg mixture
3. Cook for 1-2 minutes per side
4. When ready remove omelette from the skillet and serve

BASIL OMELETTE

Serves: **1**

Prep Time: **5** Minutes

Cook Time: **10** Minutes

Total Time: **15** Minutes

INGREDIENTS

- 2 eggs
- ¼ tsp salt
- ¼ tsp black pepper
- 1 tablespoon olive oil
- ¼ cup cheese
- ¼ tsp basil
- 1 cup red onion

DIRECTIONS

1. In a bowl combine all ingredients together and mix well
2. In a skillet heat olive oil and pour the egg mixture
3. Cook for 1-2 minutes per side
4. When ready remove omelette from the skillet and serve

CHEESE OMELETTE

Serves: *1*

Prep Time: *5* Minutes

Cook Time: *10* Minutes

Total Time: *15* Minutes

INGREDIENTS

- 2 eggs
- ¼ tsp salt
- ¼ tsp black pepper
- 1 tablespoon olive oil
- ¼ cup cheese
- ¼ tsp basil
- 1 cup mushrooms

DIRECTIONS

1. In a bowl combine all ingredients together and mix well
2. In a skillet heat olive oil and pour the egg mixture
3. Cook for 1-2 minutes per side
4. When ready remove omelette from the skillet and serve

OLIVE OMELETTE

Serves: *1*

Prep Time: 5   Minutes

Cook Time: *10*   Minutes

Total Time: *15*   Minutes

INGREDIENTS

- 2 eggs
- ¼ tsp salt
- ¼ tsp black pepper
- 1 tablespoon olive oil
- ¼ cup cheese
- ¼ cup Kalamata olives
- ¼ tsp basil
- 1 cup tomatoes

DIRECTIONS

1. In a bowl combine all ingredients together and mix well
2. In a skillet heat olive oil and pour the egg mixture
3. Cook for 1-2 minutes per side
4. When ready remove omelette from the skillet and serve

TART RECIPES

CARDAMOM TART

Serves: *6-8*

Prep Time: **25**   Minutes

Cook Time: **25**   Minutes

Total Time: **50**   Minutes

INGREDIENTS

- 4-5 pears
- 2 tablespoons lemon juice
- pastry sheets

CARDAMOM FILLING

- ½ lb. butter
- ½ lb. brown sugar
- ½ lb. almonds
- ¼ lb. flour
- 1 ¼ tsp cardamom
- 2 eggs

DIRECTIONS

1. Preheat oven to 400 F, unfold pastry sheets and place them on a baking sheet
2. Toss together all ingredients together and mix well

3. Spread mixture in a single layer on the pastry sheets
4. Before baking decorate with your desired fruits
5. Bake at 400 F for 22-25 minutes or until golden brown
6. When ready remove from the oven and serve

APPLE TART

Serves:	*6-8*	
Prep Time:	25	Minutes
Cook Time:	25	Minutes
Total Time:	*50*	Minutes

INGREDIENTS

- pastry sheets

FILLING

- 1 tsp lemon juice
- 3 oz. brown sugar
- 1 lb. apples
- 150 ml double cream
- 2 eggs

DIRECTIONS

1. Preheat oven to 400 F, unfold pastry sheets and place them on a baking sheet
2. Toss together all ingredients together and mix well
3. Spread mixture in a single layer on the pastry sheets
4. Before baking decorate with your desired fruits
5. Bake at 400 F for 22-25 minutes or until golden brown
6. When ready remove from the oven and serve

PEACH PECAN PIE

Serves: *8-12*

Prep Time: *15*   Minutes
Cook Time: *35*   Minutes
Total Time: *50*   Minutes

INGREDIENTS

- 4-5 cups peaches
- 1 tablespoon preserves
- 1 cup sugar
- 4 small egg yolks
- ¼ cup flour
- 1 tsp vanilla extract

DIRECTIONS

1. Line a pie plate or pie form with pastry and cover the edges of the plate depending on your preference
2. In a bowl combine all pie ingredients together and mix well
3. Pour the mixture over the pastry
4. Bake at 400-425 F for 25-30 minutes or until golden brown
5. When ready remove from the oven and let it rest for 15 minutes

GRAPEFRUIT PIE

Serves:	*8-12*	
Prep Time:	*15*	Minutes
Cook Time:	*35*	Minutes
Total Time:	*50*	Minutes

INGREDIENTS

- pastry sheets
- 2 cups grapefruit
- 1 cup brown sugar
- ¼ cup flour
- 5-6 egg yolks
- 5 oz. butter

DIRECTIONS

1. Line a pie plate or pie form with pastry and cover the edges of the plate depending on your preference
2. In a bowl combine all pie ingredients together and mix well
3. Pour the mixture over the pastry
4. Bake at 400-425 F for 25-30 minutes or until golden brown
5. When ready remove from the oven and let it rest for 15 minutes

Serves: **8-12**

Prep Time: **15** Minutes

Cook Time: **35** Minutes

Total Time: **50** Minutes

INGREDIENTS

- pastry sheets
- 1 package cream cheese
- 1 tsp vanilla extract
- ¼ cup peanut butter
- 1 cup powdered sugar (to decorate)
- 2 cups Butterfinger candy bars
- 8 oz whipped topping

DIRECTIONS

1. Line a pie plate or pie form with pastry and cover the edges of the plate depending on your preference
2. In a bowl combine all pie ingredients together and mix well
3. Pour the mixture over the pastry
4. Bake at 400-425 F for 25-30 minutes or until golden brown
5. When ready remove from the oven and let it rest for 15 minutes

BANANA MATCHA SMOOTHIE

Serves: **1**

Prep Time: 5   Minutes

Cook Time: 5   Minutes

Total Time: **10**   Minutes

INGREDIENTS

- 1 cup banana
- 1 tsp matcha powder
- 1 cup spinach
- 1 tsp flax seed
- 1 tsp vanilla extract
- 1 cup soy milk

DIRECTIONS

1. In a blender place all ingredients and blend until smooth
2. Pour smoothie in a glass and serve

PROTEIN SMOOTHIE

Serves: **1**

Prep Time: **5** Minutes

Cook Time: **5** Minutes

Total Time: **10** Minutes

INGREDIENTS

- 2 bananas
- 2 dates
- 1 cup kale
- 1 cup spinach
- 2 tablespoons cocoa powder
- 1 tsp vanilla extract
- 1 cup nut milk

DIRECTIONS

1. In a blender place all ingredients and blend until smooth
2. Pour smoothie in a glass and serve

CREAMY SMOOTHIE

Serves: **1**

Prep Time: **5** Minutes

Cook Time: **5** Minutes

Total Time: **10** Minutes

INGREDIENTS

- 1 cup strawberries
- 1 banana
- 1 cup Greek Yogurt
- 1 cup soy milk
- 1 tsp vanilla extract
- 1 tsp chia seeds

DIRECTIONS

1. In a blender place all ingredients and blend until smooth
2. Pour smoothie in a glass and serve

Serves: *1*

Prep Time: 5   Minutes

Cook Time: 5   Minutes

Total Time: *10* Minutes

INGREDIENTS

- 1 cup strawberries
- 1 banana
- 1 cup Greek Yogurt
- 1 scoop protein powder
- 1 tsp hemp seeds
- ½ cup chocolate chips

DIRECTIONS

1. In a blender place all ingredients and blend until smooth
2. Pour smoothie in a glass and serve

APPLE SMOOTHIE

Serves: **1**

Prep Time: **5**   Minutes

Cook Time: **5**   Minutes

Total Time: **10**   Minutes

INGREDIENTS

- 1 apple
- 2 pears
- ½ cup rolled oats
- 1 tsp cinnamon
- 1 cup nut milk

DIRECTIONS

1. **In a blender place all ingredients and blend until smooth**
2. **Pour smoothie in a glass and serve**

SPINACH SMOOTHIE

Serves: *1*
Prep Time: *5*   Minutes

Cook Time: *5*   Minutes

Total Time: *10* Minutes

INGREDIENTS

- 1 banana
- 1 cup vanilla yogurt
- 1 cup spinach
- 1 cup kale
- 1 cup orange juice

DIRECTIONS

1. In a blender place all ingredients and blend until smooth
2. Pour smoothie in a glass and serve

PEANUT BUTTER SMOOTHIE

Serves: *1*
Prep Time: 5   Minutes

Cook Time: 5   Minutes

Total Time: *10*   Minutes

INGREDIENTS

- 1 cup berries
- 2 tablespoons peanut butter
- ½ cup protein powder
- ½ cup oats
- 1 cup soy milk

DIRECTIONS

1. In a blender place all ingredients and blend until smooth
2. Pour smoothie in a glass and serve

Serves: *1*
Prep Time: *5*   Minutes

Cook Time: *5*   Minutes

Total Time: *10* Minutes

INGREDIENTS

- 1 cup pineapple
- 1 cup strawberries
- 1 cup Greek yogurt
- 1 cup soy milk
- 1 cup ice

DIRECTIONS

1. In a blender place all ingredients and blend until smooth
2. Pour smoothie in a glass and serve

Serves: **1**

Prep Time: 5   Minutes

Cook Time: 5   Minutes

Total Time: **10**   Minutes

INGREDIENTS

- 1 orange
- ½ cup orange juice
- ½ banana
- 1 tsp vanilla essence

DIRECTIONS

1. In a blender place all ingredients and blend until smooth
2. Pour smoothie in a glass and serve

RAISIN DATE SMOOTHIE

Serves: *1*
Prep Time: *5*   Minutes

Cook Time: *5*   Minutes

Total Time: *10*   Minutes

INGREDIENTS

- ¼ cup raisins
- 2 Medjool dates
- 1 cup berries
- 1 cup almond milk
- 1 tsp chia seeds

DIRECTIONS

1. In a blender place all ingredients and blend until smooth
2. Pour smoothie in a glass and serve

ICE-CREAM RECIPES

PISTACHIOS ICE-CREAM

Serves: *6-8*

Prep Time: *15*   Minutes

Cook Time: *15*   Minutes

Total Time: *30*   Minutes

INGREDIENTS

- 4 egg yolks
- 1 cup heavy cream
- 1 cup milk
- 1 cup sugar
- 1 vanilla bean
- 1 tsp almond extract
- 1 cup cherries
- ½ cup pistachios

DIRECTIONS

1. In a saucepan whisk together all ingredients
2. Mix until bubbly
3. Strain into a bowl and cool
4. Whisk in favorite fruits and mix well
5. Cover and refrigerate for 2-3 hours

6. Pour mixture in the ice-cream maker and follow manufacturer instructions

7. Serve when ready

VANILLA ICE-CREAM

Serves: *6-8*

Prep Time: *15*   Minutes

Cook Time: *15*   Minutes

Total Time: *30*   Minutes

INGREDIENTS

- 1 cup milk
- 1 tablespoon cornstarch
- 1 oz. cream cheese
- 1 cup heavy cream
- 1 cup brown sugar
- 1 tablespoon corn syrup
- 1 vanilla bean

DIRECTIONS

1. In a saucepan whisk together all ingredients
2. Mix until bubbly
3. Strain into a bowl and cool
4. Whisk in favorite fruits and mix well
5. Cover and refrigerate for 2-3 hours
6. Pour mixture in the ice-cream maker and follow manufacturer instructions
7. Serve when ready

COFFE ICE-CREAM

Serves: *6-8*

Prep Time: **15**   Minutes
Cook Time: **15**   Minutes
Total Time: **30**   Minutes

INGREDIENTS

- 4 egg yolks
- 1 cup black coffee
- 2 cups heavy cream
- 1 cup half-and-half
- 1 cup brown sugar
- 1 tsp vanilla extract

DIRECTIONS

1. In a saucepan whisk together all ingredients
2. Mix until bubbly
3. Strain into a bowl and cool
4. Whisk in favorite fruits and mix well
5. Cover and refrigerate for 2-3 hours
6. Pour mixture in the ice-cream maker and follow manufacturer instructions
7. Serve when ready

THANK YOU FOR READING THIS BOOK!

CPSIA information can be obtained
at www.ICGtesting.com
Printed in the USA
BVHW031231160321
602656BV00004B/75

9 781664 067493

A Celebration

Thomas Joseph Winning

1925 – 2001

Pope John Paul at the
elevation ceremonies
in the Vatican.

n recalling Cardinal Winning's generous and committed service as priest and bishop, I give thanks for the many blessings bestowed upon the Church through his ministry.

He was a zealous pastor who was outstanding in defence of life and commitment to the poor.

Joannes Paulus pp. II

Pope John Paul II
June 2001.

First published in Great Britain in 2001 by
MAINSTREAM PUBLISHING COMPANY (EDINBURGH) LTD
7 Albany Street
Edinburgh EH1 3UG

ISBN 1 84018 552 X

A catalogue record for this book is available from the British Library

Typeset in Garamond and Manson
Printed and bound in Great Britain by
Butler & Tanner Ltd, Frome and London

ALWAYS
WINNING

Thomas Joseph Cardinal Winning, 1925 – 2001

Fraser Elder • Martin Gilfeather • George Wilkie

MAINSTREAM
PUBLISHING

EDINBURGH AND LONDON

Thomas Joseph Cardinal Winning

June 1925 – June 2001

The story of one of the most outstanding Scots in modern history began in a working-class miner's family in Craigneuk, Lanarkshire on 3 June 1925. After a dynamic career, culminating in his being named Scotland's third cardinal since the Reformation in 1994, the final chapter was written on 17 June 2001.

Thomas Joseph Winning was initially educated at St Patrick's Primary School in Craigneuk and Our Lady's High School in Motherwell. After early training for the priesthood in Scotland he was ordained at the Pontifical Scots College in Rome in 1948.

Father Winning had earlier been one of the first three priests to be ordained for the Diocese of Motherwell and also gained pastoral experience in Chapelhall, Hamilton and Motherwell.

He returned to Rome in 1961 as Spiritual Director at the Scots College and went on to earn the title of Consistorial Advocate. He was the only secular priest in the United Kingdom qualified as an Advocate of the Rota.

On his return to Scotland in 1966, he was appointed, by Bishop Francis Thomson, Vicar Episcopal of the diocese and Parish Priest at St Luke's in Forgewood, Motherwell. Within five years, the appointment of Second Auxiliary Bishop to the Archbishop of Glasgow followed and in April 1974 he succeeded Archbishop Scanlan.

As a strong advocate of unity with other organisations and churches, he became the first Roman Catholic to address the General Assembly of the Church of Scotland in 1975.

On 26 November 1994, amid great celebrations in Rome, Pope John Paul II bestowed Thomas Joseph Winning as a cardinal priest with the title, Sant' Andrea delle Fratte, only the third Scot to achieve the honour since the Reformation.

In 1972, the Motherwell and Wishaw Council honoured the then Bishop Winning with a unique civic honour and, as Cardinal Winning in 1995, he completed a remarkable 'double' by being named a Freeman of Motherwell District, the first person to receive the accolade since the formation of the authority in 1975.

Fraser Elder

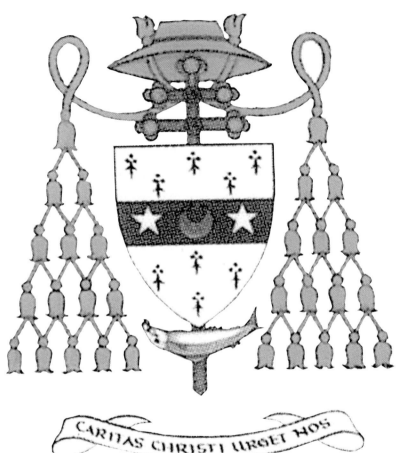

CARITAS CHRISTI URGET HOS

contents

Archbishop Winning, newly
promoted to cardinal.

HIS EMINENCE

THOMAS JOSEPH CARDINAL WINNING

1925 – 2001

3 June 1925	Born in Craigneuk, Lanarkshire
1930 – 1936	Attended St Patrick's Primary School, Craigneuk
1936 – 1942	Attended Our Lady's High School, Motherwell
1942 – 1944	Trained at St Mary's College, Blairs, Aberdeen
1944 – 1946	Studied at St Peter's College, Bearsden

1946 – 1949	Pontifical Scots College, Rome. Ordained priest 8 December1948
1949 – 1950	Assistant Priest, Chapelhall
1950 – 1953	Pontifical Scots College, Rome
1953 – 1957	Assistant Priest, St Mary's, Hamilton
1957 – 1958	Assistant Priest, Motherwell Cathedral
1958 – 1961	Chaplain to Franciscans of Immaculate Conception
1961 – 1966	Spiritual Director, Scots College, Rome
1966 – 1970	Parish Priest, St Luke's Motherwell

Nov 1971	Ordained Auxiliary Bishop of Glasgow
1972	Civic honour bestowed by Motherwell and Wishaw Town Council

April 1974	Ordained Archbishop of Glasgow
June 1982	Pope John Paul II visit to Scotland
November 1994	Created Cardinal Priest in the title of Sant' Andrea delle Fratte by Pope John Paul II
February 1995	Named Freeman of Motherwell District
17 June 2001	Died peacefully in Glasgow.

11

A contemplative Archbishop Winning sits on the beach
at Seamill, Ayrshire following the news of his promotion.

THE THOUGHTS OF
CARDINAL THOMAS WINNING

'My faith grew from a boy to a man and in every way I
sincerely hope it matured over the years.'

'The faith of the Church has become my personal faith and I
preach the faith of the Church and never my own.'

'Faith is not a vision and therefore perhaps there could be a feeling of insecurity.'

'The object of faith is Jesus Christ and is not a body of doctrines or a set of moral values.'

'It is all in the person of Jesus Christ.'

'Throughout my life I have always based everything on a foundation of three agencies . . .
family . . . school . . . and church and I have promoted the three at all times.'

'I wouldn't care to say I have all the answers. I feel if I speak with the tongues of men and
of angels and have not charity I am as St Paul said "just a sounding bell or a tinkling
cymbal". I might have the faith to move mountains and could be the greatest bishop
in the world or the greatest theologian but if I haven't got the love for the poor and
the oppressed and the compassion of Jesus Christ then I am nothing. It would be all tinsel
and all an ego trip. So I think we must find the correct balance.'

'The Church takes its agenda from the world and unless it reads the sign of the times it will
not be able to fulfil its mission the way it should.'

Thomas J. Winning

©An extract from 1994 Caledonian Television video production *The Winning Way: Prince* of *the Church, Man of the People.*

Thomas Joseph Winning, Archbishop of
Glasgow, April 1974 – November 1994

A MISCELLANY FOR A CARDINAL

I n the first half of the year 2001, the start of the new millennium, a number of great Scots were lost to the nation. While the contributions of legendary entertainers and sportsmen should never be underestimated, the most influential figure and personality to be missed will be Thomas Joseph Cardinal Winning.

From a humble start in life, on 3 June 1925 in the Lanarkshire village of Craigneuk, he rose through the ranks to become the leader of Scotland's 750,000 Roman Catholics.

As a vibrant pastor committed to many causes, he dedicated his life to improving the lives of every Scot and, through the many tributes paid to him, it is clear that he was widely regarded as a giant among church leaders and the voice of Christianity in Scotland.

He may in time be regarded as one of Lanarkshire's greatest sons, but the title of 'the Cardinal with the common touch' is his and his alone.

This was fully underlined in November 1994 when an estimated 5,000 people from all over Scotland paid their own way to Rome to make personal tributes to the one-time Scottish parish priest who became the third Scottish cardinal in history.

At the time it was overlooked that in the history of the European club football competitions, only two Scottish clubs had visited Rome: Hibernian in 1961 and Dundee United in 1984. Both clubs ultimately lost out to AS Roma and only a few hundred fans travelled from Scotland to support them – a fraction of the 'support' a miner's son from Craigneuk later commanded in the Italian capital.

Students of the English language will quickly define a miscellany as a collection of assorted writings in one book and, in paying tribute to the irrepressible Tom Winning, this publication sets out to present a celebration of his warmth and humour.

Illustrated by a huge folio of previously unpublished photographs, candid and otherwise, it is hoped to show that on a personal level and in informal situations, here was a man who was *Always Winning* and who will be quite irreplaceable.

The famous 'Mrs Mac', Isabelle MacInnes who
ran the Cardinal's household until his death.

†HE SHEPHERD

The modern archbishop can no longer be insular and lock himself away in his palace or prayer cell. Today, the priesthood is like a business, which can often mean that difficult choices have to be made by a priest who originally thought his calling was to spread the word of God.

Now, while maintaining a religious profile, he also has to become the managing director of a busy company, because that is what a diocese resembles today. A modern archbishop or bishop, as well as having to follow his religious calling, has to have the skills of an accountant, lawyer, and boardroom decision-maker in order to survive at that level.

Tom Winning had these skills and they gelled well with his religious vocation. His dual position allowed him to be heard both on religious issues and those of social deprivation. He proved his decision-making strength by cancelling a multi-million pound refurbishment of the Cathedral in Clyde Street, Glasgow, saying that the money could be better spent helping the disadvantaged in the community.

Many newspapers called him a 'troublesome priest' but he was not, he was merely fulfilling the role of a good shepherd and managing director rolled into one.

The culmination of his career was accepting the call to be a Prince of the Church. By the very nature of the position – 'to be ready to spill blood and die for the faith' – it allowed him a more powerful platform to propound his and his Church's deep beliefs.

D.H. Lawrence warned us of the able opportunist from the working class who thinks that the chief purpose of education is to enable him to put as much distance between himself and his lowly origins as he possible can. This was not so with Tom Winning.

Following his elevation he gathered his priests. Gesturing to his cardinal's ring he told them: 'This will not make any difference to me and I hope it does not to you in our relationships.' Find me a company chairman telling that to the tea lady!

Tom Winning was a veritable whirlwind. He drove everyone mad as he made sure his diary started early and finished late . . . every day! He moved from school openings to retirals, slipped in a finance meeting, attended a diocesan priests meeting, gave a TV interview, held a press conference, became MC at a dance in a hotel and then went home to watch a video. One of his former chauffeurs claimed that his wife thought he had run off because she never saw him as he was always behind the wheel.

But this was the nature of the shepherd; his flock had to be tended no matter what time of day or night.

The autograph hunters ambush the
Archbishop at a mass in Glasgow.

The lucky bidder, Martin Hughes, who paid
£5,600 for Tom Winning's zuchetto at the
Archbishop's Ball in Glasgow. Evelyn Sexton
caps the occasion with a smile.

Archbishop Winning chairs a meeting
of the Council of Priests.

Archbishop Winning with leaders of the
Muslim and Jewish faiths.

ABOVE: Archbishop Winning meets his parishioners.

BELOW: Archbishops Winning and Keith Patrick receive a science 'teach-in' from a pupil at a new Livingston school.

ABOVE: Archbishop Winning chairs a Council of Priests meeting.

BELOW: Archbishop Winning at the opening of a new school in Livingston with Lord Robertson and Robin Cook MP.

Archbishop Winning feeding
the seagulls on a beach.

A meeting of ecumenical
leaders in Scotland.

Archbishop Winning and
Archbishop Keith Patrick
O'Brien at a ceremonial service
for the Knights of Malta in Fife.

The Archbishop of Glasgow
faces the media.

1982 AND ALL THAT –

A SPECIAL REPORT BY FRASER ELDER

THE 72 HOURS THAT SAVED
THE PAPAL VISIT TO THE UK

In 1982, eight years after Thomas Winning was elevated to Archbishop of Glasgow, he was to become embroiled in some of the most intense infighting ever seen in the stately offices of the Roman Catholic curia in the Vatican.

This was to be the time when John Paul II, formerly Cardinal Wojtyla and the first-ever Polish Pope in the history of the Church, as well as being the first non-Italian for 455 years, would finally stamp his independent personality on his Church civil.

Preparations being made in Scotland for Pope John Paul's historic visit were thrown into jeopardy due to the crisis involving the Falkland Islands, Britain and Argentina. The political situation surrounding the proposed visit was straightforward in the eyes of many of his aides in the curia. In the event of the Pope carrying out his commitment to visit the United Kingdom, his action would be regarded as an insult to the nation of Argentina and, conversely, if the visit was abandoned, Britain would take great offence. The political weighting was falling on the side of Argentina and the sands of time were running out for a final decision.

The 62-year-old Pope had returned to the Vatican after a European visit that had witnessed the horror of an assassination attempt while he was in Spain. The decision over the British visit assumed cloak-and-dagger proportions as senior Roman Catholic clergy and diplomatic officials from both sides of the Atlantic shuttled to and from Rome lobbying their case.

Cardinal Gordon Gray from Scotland and Cardinal Basil Hume were both members of the British delegation which had initially attempted to convince senior Vatican advisors that the visit to Britain was essential and that the political aspects of the trip should be defused. On his return to Scotland, a very depressed Cardinal Gray openly admitted that the Church in Argentina appeared to have a strong case for preventing the tour going ahead. In an amazing seventy-two hour spell, however, Archbishop Thomas Winning of Glasgow was to emerge as the key figure in the drama, which finally resulted in the Pope stepping onto and kissing British soil. With hostilities less than a week underway in the far-off Falkland Islands, hope for a religious reconciliation between the warring clergy factions seemed to be fading. But the one-time parish priest from Craigneuk rose to the occasion and his remarkable odyssey would in time bring him one of the Church's highest honours.

In November 1994, on the eve of his installation as a cardinal priest in the title of Sant' Andrea delle Fratte, Archbishop Winning sat in his tiny hotel room on one of Rome's most fashionable streets, the Via Venito, and for the first time told the full story about the Vatican intrigues of 12 years previously.

He recalled: 'The full story of the doubts about the wisdom of the Pope's visit to Britain really started in April 1982 when the Argentinians sent their troops to the Falkland Islands and then, just days before the UK visit was scheduled, the British task force invaded the islands.

'Cardinals Basil Hume and Gordon Gray had tried extremely hard to defuse the situation in Rome but when they both returned it was obvious to all that they had not been successful – their pessimism was overwhelming as they stressed that the signs were "not good".

'During the Thursday before the planned Scottish visit, I decided to take a gamble and contacted every Roman Catholic and Christian organisation I could think of and asked them to send telegrams to the Vatican pleading with the Pope to still come to Scotland. I also sent telegrams to the cardinals in Argentina in the hope some reconciliation could be worked out.'

Not satisfied with that, Archbishop Winning also then contacted all the bishops in Scotland suggesting every one should put his name to a last-ditch plea for the UK tour to continue. With the full backing of Cardinal Gray, every bishop backed the scheme but then further help came from an unlikely source. Unknown to Archbishop Winning, a colleague and friend sitting in his house in Liverpool had been quietly doing the same thing to the clergy in England.

Winning said: 'The next day I received a call from Derek Warlock in Liverpool and he simply said "Tom, lets both of us go to Rome and see if we can sort it out! I've cleared it with my Cardinal. Why don't you do the same?"'

The Archbishop tried all day to contact Cardinal Gray by phone with no luck. He paced the room of his Glasgow home, trying every 15 minutes, and at 9 in the evening he finally made contact. The Cardinal then suggested he drive to Edinburgh immediately so they could discuss it in detail.

His driver sped him along the M8 into the leafy suburbs of Edinburgh where the two clerics sat by a dying fire until 3 a.m. discussing different points. As it was so late,

SOUVENIR of the PAPAL MASS

pope John paul II

visit to scot~ land 1982

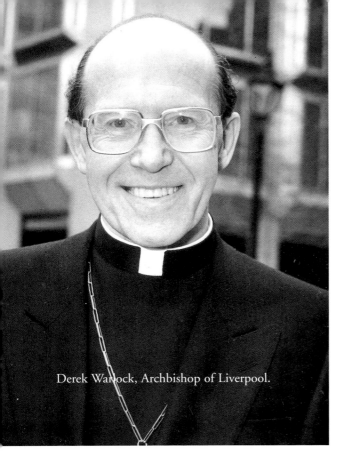
Derek Warlock, Archbishop of Liverpool.

Cardinal Gray suggested he stay the night, or what was left of it, and fly directly from Edinburgh later in the morning.

Winning said: 'We talked everything through into the early hours of Saturday morning and eventually, after many cups of tea, he suggested I make the trip to Rome. The Cardinal's parting words in the morning were to tell me that there was an air controllers' dispute in Italy and planes were being held up for hours.

'I met Derek Warlock at Heathrow airport. Somehow the media had got wind of what we were up to and we were then forced to run the gauntlet of the press.'

The two senior clerics sat for hours in the busy airport. With the clock ticking it was obvious that there was only the slimmest of chances of reaching Rome. Their chance to put their case was diminishing fast. Every avenue was being searched for a way to get them to Rome that Saturday.

While they waited, they received a mysterious call from the Italian Embassy in London which told them that, by an amazing twist of fate, an Italian Air Force plane was shortly due at Heathrow to pick up a senior Italian officer and seats would be made available to them.

They were finally on their way!

To this day no one knows who ordered that military aircraft to come to London and no Italian officer appeared for the flight. The Cardinal said: 'We were informed that the plane was supposed to be arriving to pick up an Italian Army General but in fact we never saw him and we were the only two passengers on board. It was almost like a spy thriller.'

Strapped into the spartan military plane, the crew attempted to make the two Archbishops comfortable. On top of everything else the weather had started to play up and the small plane was tossed around the sky. Said Winning: 'While we were very grateful for the lift, it turned out all we could get to drink was Coca Cola.'

They arrived at a military base 30 miles south of Rome in the early evening. From there it was a fast journey up the autostrada and into the frenetic traffic of Rome city centre. Rounds of meetings with all the parties involved began and carried on throughout the evening and well into the night, with each side lobbying as much support as possible. Up to that point they had still not met face to face.

Early on Sunday morning, Archbishops Winning and Warlock got out of their taxi at the bottom end of St Peter's Square. Too early for tourists and pilgrims, they hurried through the double line of giant stone colonnades with only the pigeons to contend with.

The early morning mists had not yet cleared the heights of the historic St Peter's Basilica. Only curia clerics in their black soutanes busily criss-crossed the square heading for their appointed offices.

They reached the first main gate guarded by Swiss Guards in their medieval dress uniforms who, on seeing them, crashed their pikes in salute. It's a well-known fact that the guards rarely remember faces or ask for security passes as they can spot cassocks made by Gammerelli tailors for senior churchmen at a hundred paces.

The two priests hurriedly made their way up the ancient cobbles around the rear of the Basilica to the curia offices. Met at the door by one of the Pope's private secretaries, they were ushered through long, never-ending corridors with high-vaulted ceilings, beautifully decorated in a simple but not austere manner, to the meeting rooms where the final decision would be made.

The only sound was their footsteps on the highly-polished wooden floor.

In the corridors and in almost all of the rooms, a clutch of Argentine clergy led by Cardinal Antonio Samore and other priests from South American countries were hard at work trying to convince the Pope's advisors to come down on their side. The two British clerics could see that they had their work cut out and got down to business.

They were greeted quite coolly but civilly by the Argentines and it was then that Archbishop Achilles Silvestrini, Assistant Secretary of State for Public Affairs, came to their assistance. Archbishop Winning recalled: 'Inside the Vatican, with lobbying going on in almost every room and corridor, it was Archbishop Silvestrini who proved to be our main ally and without question he paved the way for level-headed talks with the Argentine representatives.'

The crunch meeting began in the Pope's private office with John Paul II present. The room, painted in a deep green, was restful. There was a single wooden desk with a chair and around the room other chairs were scattered for the attending clergy. The Pope arrived and it was immediately obvious that his recent trip had physically affected him, although he strode purposefully to his desk. Behind him his aides fussed to his obvious displeasure.

The meeting ran on for a few hours but during one of the many breaks Archbishop Winning received an unexpected telegram from the unlikeliest source in Scotland. It was to become the breakthrough.

Winning said: 'While we were working feverishly against the clock to reach a decision I received a telegram from the Inter-Church Relations Committee of the Church of Scotland which was headed by the Rev. Bill Johnson. The wording was quite stunning. It read: "WE REGARD POPE JOHN PAUL II AS PROPHETIC. IF HE DOES NOT COME WE WILL NO LONGER REGARD HIM AS PROPHETIC."'

The Archbishops were called back into a meeting with the Pope and he asked if they had reached an agreement. There was muttered dissension from the South Americans. Tom Winning stepped forward and handed something to the Pope. It was the telegram he received just 30 minutes previously.

Winning recalled: 'In some awe I showed the Holy Father the message from Scotland

and I then saw in his eyes that he knew exactly what to do. All the representatives from both countries were then quickly recalled into the study and the Pope announced: "We must now lift this above politics."

'He then looked at me straight in the eye and said: "It's up to you, Monsignor, to tell me not to come, otherwise I intend to go to Britain."'

There was uproar in the room as all the Argentinian clergy began speaking at once. Still protesting they closed rapidly around the Pope who was still seated at his desk holding the telegram. The Pope's aides began to look alarmed. The two British Archbishops sat quietly.

Eventually the Argentine Cardinal raised his hand and silenced his party. He stepped close to the Pope's desk and suggested that the Holy Father should not go.

Winning said: 'The statement had caused some dismay among the Argentine delegation and a senior cardinal said that the Pope should think again and advised him to stay in Rome.'

The reply was chilling and history was about to be made.

'He told the South American Cardinal: "Thank you for your advice, but I did not ask for it."' The Pope then turned to the assembled clergy and told them of his intention to visit the UK. He then requested that all the clergy present should retire to church for a Mass of Reconciliation and heal the rift.

Derek Warlock and Tom Winning retraced their steps along the corridors. Halfway along, the Archbishop of Liverpool looked at the Archbishop of Glasgow, winked and laughed delightedly.

Within days a historic meeting with the Moderator of the Church of Scotland, the Rev. John McIntyre, was the highlight of a massive Murrayfield celebration.

On 1 June, as the Falkands conflict entered its eleventh day, the largest gathering of Roman Catholics ever seen in Scotland assembled for a memorable visit by Pope John Paul II to Bellahouston Park on the southside of Glasgow. Scots of all faiths gathered in the warm sunlight with their respective religious leaders in Glasgow's largest public park to witness a special mass conducted by the Pope. Pope John Paul II was visibly moved by the tumultuous welcome.

Fate also decreed that within two weeks of the Pope returning to Rome, the battle for the Falkland Islands had ceased.

Six months later came a sequel in the Vatican that was to touch the heart of Archbishop Thomas Winning for the rest of his life.

He said: 'Every five years archbishops are called to a gathering for the feast of St Andrew. The Pope took me aside and said "Monsignor Winning, next to visiting Poland, the welcome I received in your Glasgow and in Scotland was the warmest ever." He then beckoned me into a small private study and lying across the table was a map of Great Britain. Without hesitating he pointed to Glasgow and then put a hand across his heart and smiled broadly at me saying, "Bellahouston . . . I still have it all in here."'

Finishing, Archbishop Winning said: 'That wonderful moment told me everything and made the summer of 1982 the greatest of my life.'

British Midland flight attendant Elaine Duffy from
Glasgow managed to switch flights to be on hand

From clergy to political dignitaries to many busloads of pilgrims, the evening turned into one big ceilidh. The young Scots seminarists played hosts in their easily-identifiable purple cassocks that dated back to a time when they were described as 'the brethren who wear violet gowns'. This was a fifteenth-century 'Confraternity' of men who looked after pilgrims from Scotland, even in those days, and worked out of the Church of Sant' Andrea delle Fratte. The students crowded around the Cardinal who launched into a seminar on how to tie their waistbands without tying up themselves.

Next morning he wandered through the Parco Savallo watching the early mists rise over the Rome skyline. Then it was on to a city hospital where he visited Cathy McGee from Clydebank who had fallen and broken her hip. As he left, a mother ran to him and almost dragged him to see her young daughter who was recovering from an operation. He sat and chatted in Italian to the child, reached into his pocket and gave her his own personal rosary beads as a present. Tears ran down the cheeks of the young girl.

A special mass was said on St Andrew's Day in his church in the city. Pilgrims crowded in with the locals and shared the day with dignitaries both church and civil. The best compliments came from a short speech by the Very Reverend Professor Robert Davidson, former Moderator of the General Assembly of the Church of Scotland.

Returning home on the plane Cardinal Winning was visibly tired. On reaching Glasgow airport it was suggested to him that a few people might be there to meet him and that he should put on his red cassock. He gave his advisors a withering look and said no.

The walk from the plane to arrivals hall was quite long and as his party strolled along it was noted that the pop singer Phil Collins was in front with his minders. Turning the corner, the singer came up against a wall of newspaper photographers and television crews fronting many hundreds of Winning 'fans' who had taken over the airport.

Taken slightly aback, Collins started to ready himself for what he thought was his fan club in Scotland . . . only to be shouted at by the press to get out of the way. The look on his face was one of bemused incredulity as his place in the limelight was taken by the elderly cleric in the plain black suit.

The Man of the People – Prince of the Church was back home.

Early morning in St Peter's Square in the Vatican City.
Archbishop Winning buys a 25p bag of biscuits to feed
his favourite 'friends'. 'I do this every time I am here,
my suits are never out of the cleaners.'

Tucking into a large bowl of his favourite *pasta alla romana*, Archbishop Winning declares that if he really wanted to live somewhere in Rome it would be in the Ristorante Mariane.

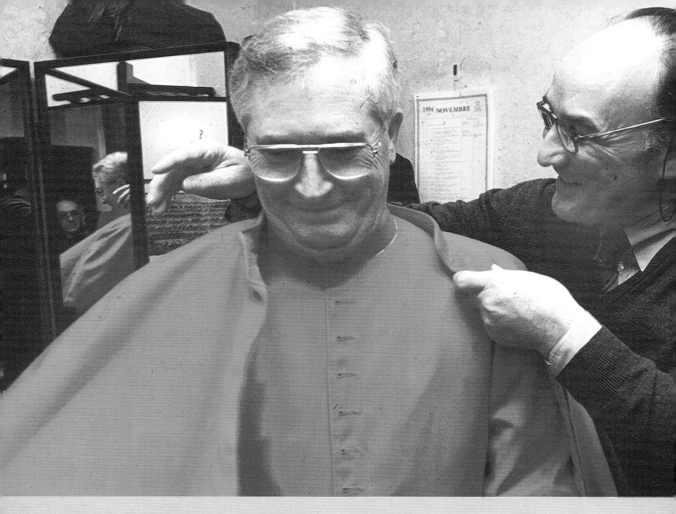

Ready for the big day and it's a visit to the top tailors for senior clergy, the Gemmerelli's, where he has the final fittings for his new 'Prince of the Church' clothes. The Archbishop said, 'I wouldn't mind but I had new bishop clothes made only six months ago here . . . I wish somebody had told me.'

Always popular, the Archbishop is frequently
stopped in the Rome streets for a chat.

On the eve of his elevation to cardinal, Tom Winning reflects on his own in the Rome church that will be designated his while he lives. During this reflection a local lady kneels before him and asks for a blessing.

The Cardinal looks over Rome
from the Lungotevere Avenito.

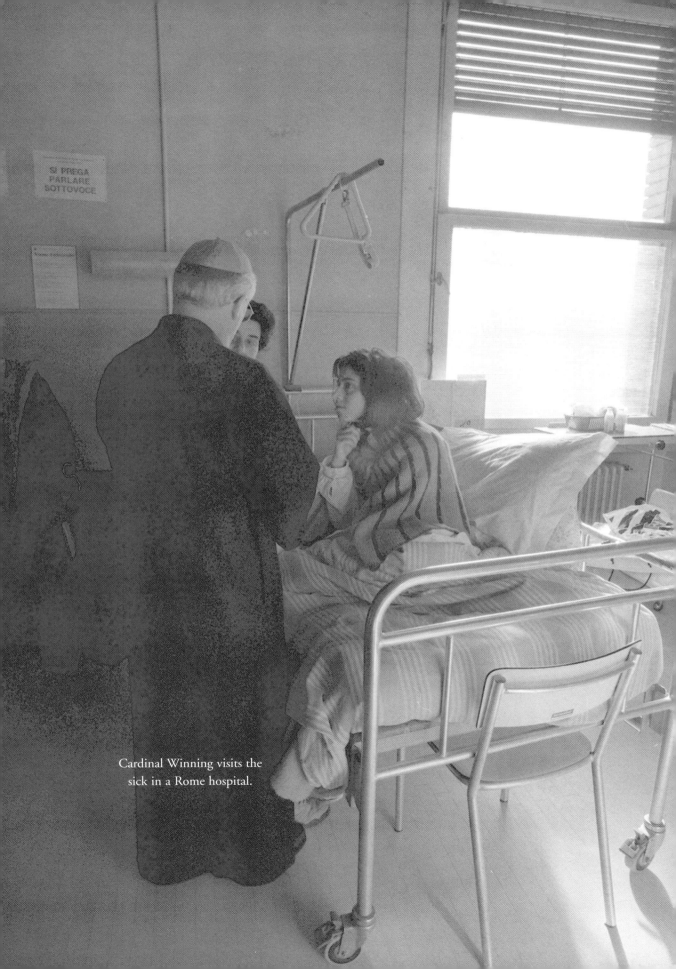

SI PREGA
PARLARE
SOTTOVOCE

Cardinal Winning visits the
sick in a Rome hospital.

ABOVE: Over a hundred priests robe in the Rome church of Sant' Andrea delle Fratte to celebrate Tom Winning becoming cardinal.

BELOW: A sea of waving white scarves as the clergy greet the new cardinals.

Cardinal Winning during the three-
hour ceremony in St Peter's Basilica in
the Vatican where he was installed as
cardinal by Pope John Paul II.

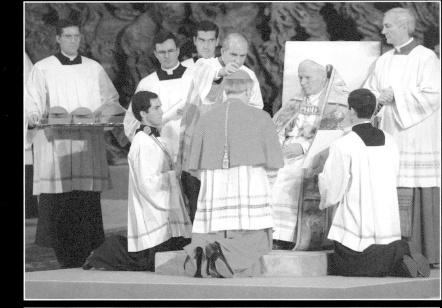

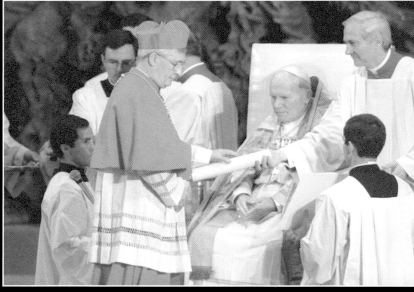

The culmination of the ceremony elevating Thomas Winning to cardinal – Prince of the Church.

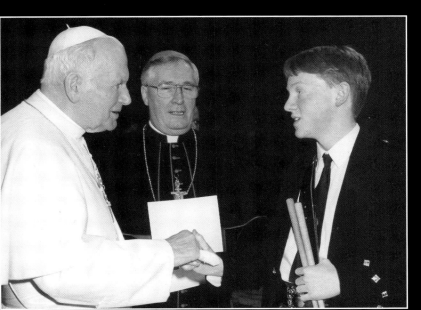

Pope John
Paul II is
introduced
to the Scots
musicians.

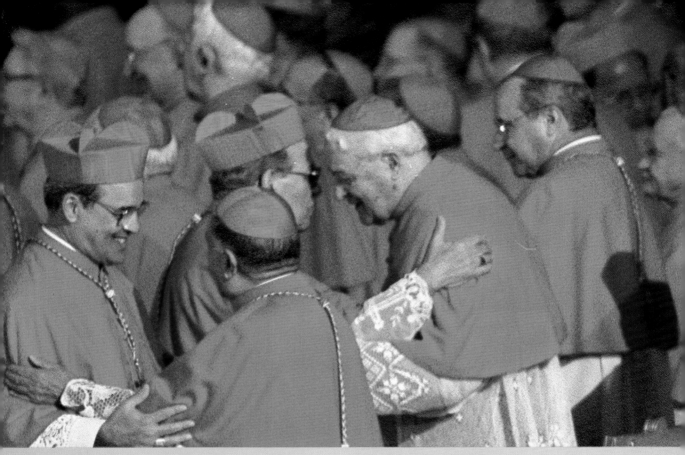

The new cardinals greet each other at a ceremony in the Vatican.

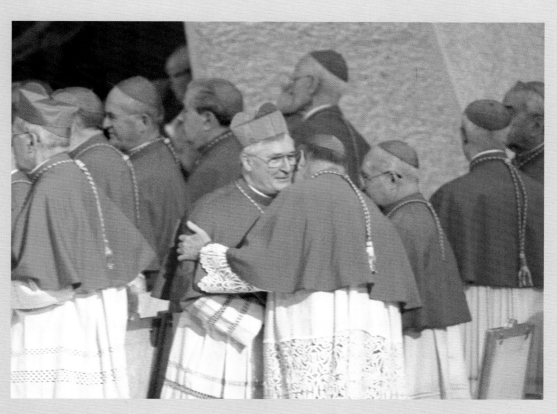

CELTIC V RAITH ROVERS

Ibrox Stadium, Glasgow, Scotland, Sunday, 27 November 1994, 5.30 p.m.
Hotel on Via Venito, Rome, Italy, Sunday, 27 November 1994, 6.30 p.m.

Over the years, Scotland's football-loving Cardinal, Thomas Winning, had little or no contact with Ibrox Stadium, the home of Celtic's greatest rivals. It was, therefore, quite ironic that the Rangers headquarters was to play a major role in a unique drama, which was enacted hundreds of miles away from Glasgow.

During the most important period of his religious career, his elevation to cardinal in the city of Rome in November 1994, Tom Winning was to miss out on a crucial engagement for Celtic FC as they set about attempting to end a success famine by securing their first major domestic trophy since 1989.

Tommy Burns and his side were pitted against Jimmy Nicholl's Raith Rovers and the authorities decreed that the Cup Final should be staged at Ibrox as Celtic were at that time based at Hampden Stadium while their own home base was under reconstruction.

Twenty-four hours earlier, Glasgow had lost an Archbishop but had gained a Cardinal and, as the Coca-Cola Cup final got under way in Scotland, a celebratory mass was being held in Rome for all newly appointed cardinals from 30 countries. Little is Cardinal Thomas Winning to know, his own home town of Motherwell would play it's own part in the high drama of the day . . .

At Ibrox, Steve Crawford opened the scoring for the Fife club and ex-Motherwell man Andy Walker levelled the score before the interval. With seven minutes remaining, Charlie Nicholas seemed to have earned Celtic their tenth League Cup success. But Motherwell-born Gordon Dalziel, the Rovers veteran skipper, sent the game into extra-time and with no further goals the game moved into a penalty showdown.

In Rome, with the day's official functions at an end, Cardinal Winning raced across the city to reach his hotel apartment in time to set up a telephone link to Glasgow as the dramatic finale got underway at Ibrox.

While the day had brought unbridled joy for one club captain, it was to bring anguish and despair for Celtic's popular skipper Paul McStay. With the score line locked at 5–5, Rovers goalkeeper Scott Thomson denied the Celtic player with a famous save and the shock waves reverberated all the way across Europe to a hotel room in Rome.

Cardinal Winning after his elevation. He
meets some of the many Scots pilgrims
who came to the ceremony.

The celebrations begin in
the streets of the Vatican City.

ABOVE: Cardinal Winning with some of the young trainee priests who attend the Scots College in Rome

BELOW: Cardinal Winning with Croatian nuns who looked after him as a trainee priest.

A celebration mass at his appointed Rome church
Sant' Andrea delle Fratte.

Cardinal Winning and all his relatives at lunch in Rome.

Cardinal Winning arrives home from Rome at Glasgow airport.

ABOVE: Cardinal Winning with Lord George Robertson of NATO and Dr John Reid, Secretary of State for Northern Ireland.

BELOW: Winning talks with curia powerbrokers in the Vatican.

ABOVE: Cardinal Winning runs the media gauntlet.

BELOW: Meeting old friends at the Gregorian University.

Cardinal Winning at the SECC, Glasgow.

Overwhelmed by the greetings from his
fans at Glasgow airport.

The never-ending
lines of well-wishers
at the party in the
Scots College of
Rome.

Piper Mark Lunny leads pilgrims into the Vatican.

A CELEBRATION BY

ARCHBISHOP KEITH PATRICK O'BRIEN

I have so many happy memories of visits by Cardinal Winning and of his friendship with many people whose stories he was always interested in hearing.

I remember one of our senior priests was celebrating the Golden Jubilee of his ordination to the priesthood and I was approached by the committee organising the event and asked if Cardinal Winning should be invited. Obviously I had no objections, but I provided an 'excuse' for him by saying he would be so busy, not only with the responsibilities of his own archdiocese, but in Rome and other parts of the world.

When I advised the Cardinal of this he immediately said, 'But Keith, I want to go there! Some years ago my housekeeper, Mrs Mac, was at a mass celebrated by that priest and at it he spoke very kindly of me and my first words as a visitor to the General Assembly of the Church of Scotland. This is a way in which I can repay him!'

Friendship and respect for people of all faiths and none was a mark of the Cardinal's ministry as priest, bishop and cardinal.

I know that he took his position as parish priest of Sant' Andrea delle Fratte very seriously and in a concerned way. I remember receiving a letter from someone who had revisited this church the day before the Cardinal was to say another mass. The church was full of activity with flower arrangers, cleaners and others who were organising posters and leaflets. Many young children and older people were helping amid a great buzz of excitement. Of the many parishioners who were there, almost everyone had met the Cardinal and spoken with him. He knew their families and even relatives living beyond the city. They spoke with such pride and affection for '*Il nostro Cardinale*' that the Scots who listened were very moved but not at all surprised.

'The man with the common touch, concerned for all', does indeed very adequately describe Cardinal Thomas Winning.

Archbishop Keith Patrick O'Brien is Archbishop of St Andrews and Edinburgh.

Scots entertainer Andy Cameron wears Cardinal
Winning's red zuchetto before auctioning it at the
Cardinal's Ball, 1996.

A CELEBRATION BY

ANDY CAMERON

This was the man who was the Prince of his Church, the leading Catholic in Scotland, but at no time did he ever lose the common touch of a working-class lad from Lanarkshire.

The first time I met T.J. was while I was performing my cabaret spot for his Charity Ball in the then Albany Hotel in Glasgow.

In the middle of my act, in which I was wearing a suit that was halved in blue and green, he walked across the floor and asked, 'Where did you get THAT suit?'

Before I could stop myself, I pointed to his cassock and quipped: 'You're no' that well dressed yersel goin' about wi' a frock on!'

I suddenly realised what I had said but, before I could become embarrassed, he laughed heartily, patted me on the shoulder and then returned to his seat.

From that moment on I knew I had met a man of the people.

I was always completely at ease in his company and I could see that he made everyone else feel very comfortable whenever they joined him.

Several years after that first meeting I was doing another stint at another charity event which had by then been changed from the Archbishop's Ball to the Cardinal's Ball, and as usual he took the floor for the vote of thanks. As he joined me, to thank me, he took off his red cap of office and stuck it on my head, then shook us all by saying 'See how much you can raise for that in your auction!'

Almost unbelievably, I managed to raise five thousand six hundred pounds for the cap and afterwards I asked him how we could possibly top that at the next ball the following year.

'No bother,' was T.J.'s reply 'I'll get you a cap from his Holiness the Pope!'

And believe it or not he did just that! I really don't know who was more delighted the next year when we raised a remarkable twenty-six thousand pounds for the Holy Father's bunnet!

Sadly Tom Winning is no longer with us and I for one will miss him very much. The smile when his eyes lit up and always the look of joy when he held a child in his arms are wonderful memories to recall. Even all the wind-ups when his team Celtic defeated my favourites, Rangers. These are all great memories and I sincerely hope the fund of stories and images in this book will help us all remember with fondness – a fine human being.

Andy Cameron is a Scottish entertainer and broadcaster.

Not everyone is impressed by the presence
of an Archbishop in their church.

A CELEBRATION BY

THE RIGHT HON. ALEX MOSSON

Much has been said and written about the late Cardinal Thomas Winning in recent times and I would like to add to all the fine tributes by stressing just how much he meant to me and the people of Glasgow.

Since becoming a councillor in 1984 I had the privilege to meet him on many occasions and he always came over as someone who cared very much for people. I always admired his natural ability to welcome every person from all walks of life.

He was greatly admired for his forthright approach and his determination to promote the teachings of the Roman Catholic faith and ensure that the Christian family of churches were more involved and worked with each other.

In May 2001, at the Civic Mass held in Our Lady and St George's Church in Penilee in Glasgow, he firmly emphasised the need for the Churches and the City Council to work together for a better society and a stronger community spirit. I am more than confident that Glasgow City Council will continue to work towards this end.

It was common knowledge that Cardinal Winning had a wonderful sense of humour and my wife and I shared some fun with him during a visit to Bethlehem.

During the Holy Land Pilgrimage, my wife was wearing a navy-blue dress and jacket with gold piping. The Cardinal was well aware that she had attended Garnethill Girls School in Glasgow as a young girl and he remarked, 'Tell me. Is that your school blazer you're wearing?'

There are so many stories about his sense of fun and that gives an insight into the Cardinal's approach to life. He will be remembered for his sincerity and forthrightness and his 'man of the people' style.

He is sadly missed.

The Right Hon. Alex Mosson LL.D. O. St J. is Lord Provost of Glasgow.

A CELEBRATION BY

FATHER JOHN MORRISON

y arrival in the '70s as an assistant governor at Barlinnie Prison in Glasgow coincided with Archbishop Winning's first pastoral visit. The Governor at the time could never be described as a 'Roman' sympathiser, nor as a man imbued with a zeal for penal reform, and this particular visit was a serious challenge to his tolerance for the Church and compassion for delinquents. The day turned out to be most eventful!

At the outset the Archbishop was met by the No. 2 Chief Officer and escorted into the presence of the Governor and his No. 1 Chief as if he was a member of the Royal Family.

The Governor's idea of a pastoral visit was somewhat different to that of the visiting priest. In the case of the former, it meant that no prisoner should get within 100 yards of the honoured guest. For the latter, it was an opportunity to have a hands-on meeting with them and I suspect neither knew the other's agenda. Thus, a battle of wits unfolded.

The episcopal procession through the workshops, hospital and cellblocks was carried out without a hitch. A sanitised sweep of senior officers ensured no 'contamination' by prisoners, except the selected few of compliant behaviour.

The Governor was most pleased with the success of his programme and gave the impression he was almost on the point of conversion to the Faith when . . . disaster struck!

As the party walked through C Hall, a voice from the first landing rang out: 'How's it going Tom?'

Such a cry would demand an example be made and a serious punishment would certainly follow for the prisoner foolish enough to be so familiar with a dignitary. Tom looked up at the caller and immediately set off up the stairs where he was invited into the cell without the benefit of an escort guard. Around 15 minutes later, the Archbishop emerged from the cell with first names being exchanged in an animated conversation. Such familiarity by a prisoner was another offence so further punishment was pending.

Without fuss the Archbishop turned to the astounded Governor and the group and explained that he had lived in the same street as the prisoner when they were boys and meeting up with him again had made his day at the 'Bar L'.

Father John Morrison is Parish Priest of Loanhead. He is former Asst. Governor of Barlinnie Prison and former Governor of Wormwood Scrubs.

Saturday morning and Archbishop Winning
walks in his garden in Glasgow.

A CELEBRATION BY

BRIAN DEMPSEY

When Father Thomas Winning was appointed parish priest at St Luke's in Motherwell, it was soon apparent that he was very much a disciple of the Second Vatican Council.

Thus it was, as a native of Sacred Heart, Bellshill, I first came to meet the young priest, not so much because of the force of his personality, but because he trail-blazed what was then an innovative – and convenient – Vigil Mass.

He was not unknown to my family, particularly my late father, James Dempsey MP. Their paths had crossed when Father Winning served as Motherwell's Diocesan Secretary for Bishop James Donald Scanlan and even then it was apparent this was a priest who would go places.

By the late '80s we came into closer personal contact when he invited me to advise on developing a fund-raising strategy to raise one million pounds for good causes before the end of the millennium. He had already earned a firm reputation as an outspoken church leader and was ever ready to voice his opinion and his church's opinion on a multitude of issues. Although it was a style of leadership that attracted as many critics as admirers, no one could ever suggest he was merely posturing.

On a one-to-one basis his geniality was particularly evident. So too was the pugnacious strand in what was undoubtedly a complex personality.

A bishop since 1971, and acutely media-conscious, he had become well acquainted with wielding authority. Perhaps unwittingly, the Director of the Pro-Life Initiative captured what seems to have been the key aspect of his leadership style as she simply described him as 'The Boss!'

He WAS the Boss, and he knew it!

In-depth analyses of his colourful personality and of his tenure as Glasgow's longest serving post-Reformation archbishop and first cardinal will no doubt follow in due course. What is so immediately evident is the fact we shall not see his like again.

In my last conversation with Cardinal Winning he was then, as I will always remember him, polemical in character, energetic, ebullient and perceptive.

May he rest in peace.

Brian Dempsey is a well-respected entrepreneur and businessman.

A celebration mass at his appointed
Rome church Sant' Andrea delle
Fratte with his Scots bishops.

A CELEBRATION BY

THE RIGHT REV. JOSEPH DEVINE

I take particular pride in making this contribution in tribute to Cardinal Thomas Winning as he was a son of Lanarkshire from Shieldmuir or Craigneuk. (The name was dependent on the faith tradition of the residents, as the 'Tims' called it Shieldmuir and the 'Billies' used the other title!)

In his 52 years as a priest, he served in his native diocese for only 20 years in parishes in Chapelhall, Hamilton and Motherwell, while also being on the staff of his beloved Scots College in Rome from 1961 to 1966.

One of his proudest memories came when the former Motherwell and Wishaw District Council installed him as a Freeman of Motherwell in 1972, only the third son of the area to receive such an honour following in the footsteps of Sir Alexander Gibson and Professor Willie Barclay. Due to changes in local government, no other person will receive such a distinction.

Known to but a few is the fact his surname was not Winning but Wynne! When his grandfather fell victim to the Irish famine he sought employment in Scotland where a local foreman was unable to spell the surname and entered the name Winning. It was a happy error as in time the grandson of the family was to prove himself forever winning.

Thomas Joseph Cardinal Winning was the superstar of the Catholic Church in the latter part of the twentieth century. He was most admired by the Catholic community of Scotland and particularly by the priests and members of the Archdiocese of Glasgow for two reasons. The first was his defence of traditional moral values and, whether people agreed or disagreed, it was not possible to ignore him. The second was his ready wit and sense of humour.

Years ago at the end of the Papal Mass in Bellahouston Park, as the Pope was being conveyed in the popemobile to his helicopter, the crowd sang 'Will ye no' come back again.' Thomas Joseph attempted to explain in fluent Italian that the song was a tribute to Bonnie Prince Charlie but found he could not translate the words Bonnie and Charlie. The Pope then heard him say the crowd were singing about Prince Charles and he said. 'Ah yes, I met his mother in London last Thursday!' The Cardinal loved to tell the story against himself as he was never a man to stand on his dignity.

The Right Rev. Joseph Devine is Bishop of Motherwell.

Archbishop Winning catches a few
moments of relaxation in his library.

A CELEBRATION BY

MICHAEL MARTIN MP

y first ever meeting with Thomas Winning came when he was ordained auxiliary bishop in November 1971 by Archbishop Scanlan, and from that very first moment I was more than convinced this would be a man who would make an enormous impact and reach the highest level in church affairs in Scotland and over a wider canvas.

In the 20 years that have subsequently passed, when he served as Auxiliary Bishop, Archbishop of Glasgow and the highest accolade as Cardinal, I was privileged to attend the many services and functions in which he was the officiating clergyman, and at such times he carried out his duties with a great warmth and dignity.

He thrived on the informality after these commitments and was always at his best in the church hall afterwards, where he took time out to speak to every parishioner and visitor in an extremely jovial manner.

One of my favourite memories of the man who later became Cardinal Thomas Winning involved a Saturday engagement when he was involved in the consecration of a new church, and the service and official proceedings were scheduled to last several hours.

During the afternoon his favourite football team, Celtic of course, were in action at their home in the east end of Glasgow. Prior to the start of the service he approached me with a huge smile on his face and a twinkle in his eye and said: 'Michael, it would appear I will be more than tied up here for the next few hours but I will be depending on you to keep me fully informed as to what the score is at Parkhead!'

Michael Martin is Member of Parliament for Springburn and Speaker of the House of Commons.

Cardinal Winning overlooking Rome
in the Parco Savallo.

A CELEBRATION BY

MARTIN GILFEATHER

Over the years my impression of Cardinal Thomas Winning was of him being the original enigma. But by lifting that curtain, you could establish that he was a very complex mixture of human being: a statesman of the clergy and a true football fan. Each being part and the whole of his persona.

Having said that, I found that he could put anyone at ease immediately, while still retaining an observant perception of him or her. His ability to flow through all these different levels was highly impressive. From chatting in the streets of Rome to colleagues to being dragged by the hand of a worried Italian mother to visit her child in hospital, he took it all in his stride.

As a professional photographer, the main pleasure for a 'Winning watcher' like me was studying his eyes as he conducted his emotions and feelings through them – they were his physical charisma. Without doubt, he had a worldwide fan following which could easily have matched any superstar's from the entertainment world.

Recently, I met a lady in New Brunswick in Canada who was an important member of her community. Following a short chat she moved on, only to return to berate me for not telling her I knew Cardinal Thomas Winning. For the remainder of my visit, at least over an hour and to the total exclusion of everyone else, we reminisced about the magic of the Cardinal.

His sense of humour was legendary, always inescapable and ever bubbling to the surface.

One day at Heathrow Airport a friend of mine who had not crossed paths with him for several years, approached him with hand outstretched and said: 'Your Grace . . .'

Said the Cardinal, pointing at him: 'Ralph Slater . . .'

'No,' said my friend rather bemused, 'I'm Barry Evans from Newlands, Your Grace.'

The Cardinal said: 'The suit, Barry. It's definitely from Ralph Slater's as I have got one similar!'

To sum up Cardinal Thomas Joseph Winning to anyone in just a few words, I would always describe him with fondness as being 'a very, very, BIG wee man'.

Martin Gilfeather is a photojournalist.

A sea of red scarves as the the new
cardinals await their elevation.

A CELEBRATION BY

GRAHAM SCOTT

orking in what was then titled the Clydebank Press in the late '60s was more than a worthwhile learning experience for an aspiring journalist. It was a vibrant time when the town, thriving with its famous shipyards and sewing-machine works, also had a personality as a parish priest at Our Holy Redeemer's Church . . . a certain Father Thomas Winning.

His good works and his sense of humour were ever evident. He was even accorded the ancient title of 'Bankie of the Year' on one occasion and celebrated the accolade at a function in the old Yoker Athletic FC Social Club.

Father Winning's real humour shone through like a beacon one time and it involved one of the great characters of the journalistic world in Scotland, the late Bob Ramsey.

Along with Bob, a converted Roman Catholic, who was the editor of the Clydebank publication, this young up-and-coming writer sometimes enjoyed excessive liquid lunch hours of a Friday in the town's Burgh Bar. On returning to the office after one such social session we were relaxing suitably when two Mormon missionaries called in. The eloquent Ramsey, an intellectual wit as well as a religious believer, told them he wasn't remotely interested in their cause but was most anxious to help them spread the gospel elsewhere.

After scribbling on a piece of paper, he told the two rather naïve Americans: 'Take yourselves along to this address in Glasgow Road and when you get there just ask for Big Tam and tell him Bob Ramsey sent you.' The two Mormons sped off, convinced they had a new recruit. The address, of course, was the priest's house at Our Holy Redeemer's Church!

After Mass the following Sunday, Ramsey found a note pinned to the church noticeboard 'inviting' him along for a chat with the only 'Big Tam' to become a cardinal in later life.

Graham Scott is a journalist living and working in Glasgow.

Cardinal Winning and Archbishop J. Foley,
the President of the Pontifical Council for
Social Communion.

A CELEBRATION BY

THE MOST REV. JOHN P. FOLEY

The late and much-lamented Cardinal Thomas Joseph Winning had a truly marvellous sense of humour and I remember most fondly him enjoying some fun and laughing so hard the tears were rolling down his cheeks!

I was visiting Glasgow with Cardinal Winning's good friend, Bishop Joseph Devine of Motherwell, and it was also the occasion when the former Papal Nuncio Archbishop Barbarito, previously the Nuncio in Australia, was in Scotland.

Cardinal Winning asked him: 'Your Grace, would you like a light breakfast tomorrow morning?'

Archbishop Barbarito, mistaking the word 'light' for an Australian pronunciation of 'late' replied with a straight face: 'No, I'd prefer to eat early!'

The then Archbishop of Glasgow doubled over in laughter and the tears flowed down his face while the rest followed suit and laughed at both the misunderstanding and Tom Winning's reaction. The poor Nuncio sat there baffled. He must have wondered 'What have I said?' Even when everything was explained, I have the feeling Archbishop Barbarito was unable to grasp the humour of the situation. For me, that summed up Cardinal Winning who was direct, spontaneous and quick to appreciate the sense of humour of a situation.

Although he was a refreshingly simple man, Cardinal Winning once told me he was very proud and grateful for three things: to be a Roman Catholic, to be a priest and to be a Scot.

Being a cardinal did not change him one bit, in fact, it made his delightful personality better known in a wider world and made him more universally loved.

May his great soul rest in the Peace of the Lord whom he loved and served so well.

(The Most Rev.) John P. Foley is Titular Archbishop of Neapolis in Proconsulari and President of the Ponitifical Council for Social Commmunications. He is based in the Vatican.

Lord Robertson and Robin
Cook MP, together with
Cardinal Winning, receive a
lesson in new technology.

A CELEBRATION BY

JAMES McFAUL MP

Honest, direct, modest, young at heart and monumentally committed to his cause. These are my reflections on the life of the late Cardinal Thomas Joseph Winning.

A Prince of the Church? – the regal description left him feeling uncomfortable. He was more at home at the local parish bingo night than in the splendid surroundings of the Vatican.

Education was the key to his liberation from the poverty-ridden environment of 1940s Lanarkshire. He grabbed it with both hands and used it to such stunning effect. If he hadn't pursued his religious vocation, I could imagine him as a radical QC, lecturing a judge on the poverty of opportunity experienced by his client. Addressing the judge he would have said: 'My Lord, but for the grace of God, you could have been in my client's position – so for God's sake gie him a break!'

I also think that he would have been equally successful as a left-wing MP: exiled to the backbenches, intolerant of the status quo, the bane of the establishment.

He was a voice in the wilderness at times, a prophet and guardian of the poor people's interests, but he always had a smile and a mischievous sense of humour and it's the latter I remember most clearly.

I recall an event at a school in Dumbarton when, talking to a group of young people, I asked one individual what career he wanted to pursue: 'I have half a mind to be a politician,' the boy said. Quick as a flash, T.J. retorted: 'Aye and that is all you need to be a successful politician!'

A comedian and a cardinal all rolled into one – what a brew!

May he rest in peace.

John McFaul MP is Member of Parliament for Dumbarton.

The Very Rev. Professor Davidson pays
tribute to the new Cardinal Winning in
the Sant' Andrea delle Fratte.

A CELEBRATION BY

THE VERY REV. W.B. JOHNSTON, DD.D LITT.

I remember Tom Winning as a congenial companion and a doughty theologian.

At a time when I was the Church of Scotland's Convenor of the Inter-Church Relations Committee we met up one month on the lovely west coast island of Iona – a place of pilgrimage and meditation for all Christian faiths.

One morning we had a companionable walk together across the island and our discussion during the walk became pretty animated – it was about the content of a sermon preached that morning by the Rev. George McLeod and Tom took some exception to its content. I found myself (unusually) defending George, but Tom would have none of it. On this occasion we didn't have a Bible with us to refer to – Tom was a terrible man for borrowing mine! However, we agreed to disagree and continued to take in the wonderful Scottish island scenery. When I got home to Edinburgh I looked up the matter in contention and, of course, Tom was right!

When the uncertainty surrounded the visit by Pope John Paul II to Britain during the Falklands war, Tom went to the Vatican, along with Derek Warlock of Liverpool, to attempt to persuade him not to cancel – a visit by the two clerics, which one of my priest friends said, was of two priests who 'shoot from the hip'. We sent him a message at that time which we hoped would be of help and support for their cause.

I, and my friends in the Church of Scotland, shall miss Tom for his humour and sagacity as well as for his friendship and ecumenical cooperation.

The Very Rev. W.B. Johnston DD. D Litt. is former Convenor of the Church of Scotland Inter-Church Relations Committee.

Archbishop Winning meets a group
of ecumenical leaders in Glasgow.

A CELEBRATION BY

DR MICHAEL KELLY

My links with Cardinal Thomas Winning stretched over 50 years and, from humble beginnings in Hamilton, our association built to a peak with the historic visit of Pope John Paul II to Glasgow in 1982.

While he was the Bishop of Motherwell's secretary, I invited him to join me in a round of golf and after signing him in at the local club, Bothwell Castle, I realised I had only ever addressed him as Dr Winning and had absolutely no idea what his Christian name was. The look he gave me when he answered 'Tom' made it very clear that, although we were about to play a friendly game of golf, the formalities between the clergy and the laity were not to be brushed aside!

Along with my wife Zita, I was privileged to meet the then Archbishop Winning during our honeymoon in Rome in 1966 and I marvelled at the way he had become fully integrated into the Roman way of life. Crushed into his little Fiat car, his ability to follow the doctrine 'When in Rome etc.' and shout and gesticulate was an education. He summed things up saying, 'It's the only way you will survive in this traffic.'

Given that we had known each other for such a long period, it was a remarkable coincidence that our paths met in such a dramatic fashion in 1982 while planning the first Papal visit to Glasgow in the history of the Roman Catholic Church. Tom Winning was the Archbishop of the city and I held the position of Lord Provost. The local authority, with Jean McFadden as Council Leader, worked tirelessly to make certain the big day at Bellahouston Park was a credit to the city and Scotland in general. While there were bouts of political infighting, red tape was effectively cut behind the scenes to make the correct things happen.

One drama involved a beech hedge at the park, which was apparently blocking the proposed route from the helicopter pad to the specially built altar. The evening before the visit, the Council Leader authorised a suitable gap to be cut in the hedge and then she phoned me, clearly to hand me some of the responsibility – or blame!

The next day, while waiting with the Archbishop for the helicopter, I drew his attention, with a certain amount of tongue in cheek, to the gaping hole in the historic hedge. He made no comment and I still presume he never knew the big risks to certain political reputations that had been taken to make sure his big day ran smoothly.

Dr Michael Kelly CBE is former Lord Provost of Glasgow 1980–84.

I first got to know the future Cardinal when we were both pupils at Our Lady's High School in Motherwell. He was from St Patrick's parish and I hailed from St Cuthbert's in Burnbank, Hamilton.

When we realised that we both had ambitions to be priests we became firm friends, successfully surviving the short interviews by a formidable panel of elderly clerical dignitaries in the Renfrew Street headquarters of the Archdiocese of Glasgow. Tom was 17 years of age, I was 16 and we were both pronounced suitable to be accepted as students for the priesthood.

On an August afternoon in 1942, we bade farewell to our parents on a platform at Buchanan Street railway station. I never found out if Tom was as nervous or homesick as I was when we finally reached Blairs College in Aberdeen.

Blairs was the national junior seminary and, because of the wartime closure of the two senior seminaries in Rome and Valladolid, St Peter's College in Bearsden was full with 'theologians' – the seminarians in their final four years of preparation. Therefore, the 'philosophers' – those of us in our first two years of our post-Highers studies – were given accommodation at Blairs.

Our rooms were cubicles with a curtain as a door and, with the food monotonous and totally predictable, we were nutritionally 'challenged'. However, we were quite happy for the two years, even if we could not unconditionally subscribe to the claim of the College song: 'Joys of home . . . how sweet forever, can't compare with those of Blairs'!

Tom and I parted as I served three years military service and we met again when I was sent to the Scots College in Rome in 1947. By that time Tom had moved well ahead of me in his preparation for the priesthood.

We remained friends as priests, although never close as our paths took different directions. But when I was made a bishop in 1981, our friendship became very close and, at my invitation, he preached when I was ordained in the grounds of Fatima House, Coodham.

Even more moving for me was the Mass of Chrism during Holy Week in the Good Shepherd Cathedral in Ayr in 1994. I was recovering from a serious eye operation at the time and as I could hardly see, let alone read, I was unable to be the principal celebrant of the Mass. Archbishop Winning immediately offered his help.

During the service and at the moment when the bishop asks the assembled priests of the diocese to renew their commitment of faithful service, which is always an emotional experience for me, the Archbishop handed me the text and somehow I struggled through the words, deeply moved and immensely grateful for his thoughtfulness.

When he became cardinal, he made visits to every Scottish diocese, Galloway included. We had a joyful mass in our cathedral and later he spent hours meeting and greeting the long queues of people who wanted to speak to him. He thrived on that kind of situation and any previously arranged schedule had to be abandoned.

In 1997, Galloway marked the sixteenth centenary of St Ninian's arrival in Scotland and, led by the Cardinal, the Scottish bishops were present at the Whithorn pilgrimage.

On the long way down to St. Ninian's cave, everyone had a tiring walk along a very muddy path to the pebbled beach. To make matters worse, the rain was simply pouring down. When the Cardinal arrived, to great applause, he made a rather incongruous figure wearing old waterproof trousers and a pair of green wellies appropriated from sympathetic parishioners. Fortunately the rain ceased as mass began and after a 'dry' liturgy we had a less arduous return to Whithorn.

The Cardinal was always happy at the seaside and he used the Seamill Hydro in Ayrshire on many occasions for planning meetings and bishops' in-service gatherings. It is so poignant that he had arranged to spend a few weeks in Seamill during the period of his convalescence, which had been decreed by his doctors. Alas, due to his second and fatal heart attack the visit never came to pass.

May he now be enjoying infinitely greater rest and happiness in Heaven.

The Right Rev. Maurice Taylor is Bishop of Argyll and the Isles.

A CELEBRATION BY

BILLY McNEILL

I was truly privileged to have known Thomas Winning, later to become a cardinal, from the time I was a secondary schoolboy at Our Lady's High School in Motherwell and he was an assistant priest in St Mary's in Hamilton. In later years we became close friends when we became neighbours in the Newlands area of Glasgow. As a result of this I was able to meet him and enjoy his company quite regularly away from the many formal occasions and ceremonies he had to attend.

Knowing this remarkable man over such a lengthy period, I was always convinced he would rise and grow in position in the church and he fully deserved the title of being a man of the people.

Of course, with my lengthy association with Celtic FC as a player and then a manager, a great many people have asked me about Cardinal Winning's great love for the club and the humour which can only surround such an eminent figure being a football fan.

His visits to Celtic games were countless, but my greatest recollection of the Cardinal and a football game took place well away from Parkhead, and on that occasion he certainly got the better of me!

It involved a serious Church function in Glasgow one Sunday afternoon and, just by chance, Celtic was to be playing in a live game on television. The then Archbishop of Glasgow collared me before the festivities began with a plan to get to a TV screen. He said: 'I will get through my part of the ceremony as smartly as possible and then you and I can settle down somewhere to see the game!'

He was good as his word and after his contribution he gave me the nod and left the top table. Unfortunately, before I could make my move from the main area, the Archbishop of St Andrews and Edinburgh got to his feet and started what turned out to be quite a lengthy speech and out of respect I had to sit tight – so I missed the game.

Later I told the Cardinal what had happened and said to him that only people with his kind of authority could work wonders. He just smiled!

He was a fine person to know and somehow I do have the feeling he was so committed in his support for Celtic he would have loved to have spent the bulk of his time following the team everywhere.

Billy McNeill MBE, Celtic FC 1957–75. Club Manager 1978–83, 1987–91.

Archbishop Winning wanders through the many stalls
selling garden produce in the back streets of Rome.

A CELEBRATION BY

EILEEN A. MILLAR

hen Italians want to describe someone who is likeable, friendly and kindly they say: '*è molto simpatico*'. This phrase has a depth of meaning which is instantly understood but difficult to translate into simple words and the same could be said of Cardinal Winning. So many people have written and spoken about his easy manner and winning smile, but if those characteristics had more than superficial value, they had to spring from a person whose depth of humanity and spirituality gave him that natural assurance to be himself, whatever the situation. While small incidents can sometimes reveal these qualities more clearly than large gestures or statements, more importantly, they demonstrate that there was no dichotomy between the private and the public persona of the Cardinal.

As a young research student in Rome, I well remember my delight when he phoned me one morning in my modest *pensione* to find out how I was getting on and invite me for a meal. In those days, it was an enormous treat to be taken out to a 'real' Roman restaurant and just before he hung up, he asked: 'By the way, do you need any money, hen?' I hastened to reassure him of my financial solvency, but I was deeply struck by his sensitivity and spontaneous generosity.

These were the same endearing, human qualities which radiated the empathy and warmth that touched so many people. These attributes were woven into his personality from his earliest years through his family, school and parish life. He never lost sight of his roots and the more responsibility he was given, the more sympathetic he became to human need. No one was too insignificant for his attention; he had a passionate love for people and their needs and felt deeply responsible before God, particularly because of the position he had been given.

Eileen A. Millar is Stevenson Professor of Italian at the University of Glasgow.

A CELEBRATION BY

THE RIGHT REV. JOHN MONE

My first memories of Cardinal Winning spring from my friendship with him as brother priest and brother bishop when I was, for a few years, his Auxiliary Bishop.

It says a great deal that one of the roles I took upon myself, when I celebrated mass with him, was to make certain he switched off his radio microphone in case some of his humorous asides were picked up by the congregation and heard 'out of context'.

His friendship and support were very important to me after I became Bishop of Paisley. I invited him to the diocese on several occasions and his visits were always memorable. He made them so! He told me he was always delighted to come as he was always made to feel so welcome and felt at home amongst his extended family.

In February 1995 we welcomed him to the diocese for the first time as Cardinal with a mass in St Mirin's Cathedral. He spoke informally to us and told us he was wearing the vestments Pope John Paul II had used at the mass in Bellahouston Park during his memorable visit. He spoke of the links with the Holy Father and the need to be loyal and close to him.

His last visit to the diocese was very special to him for personal as well as Church reasons, as Bishop McGill celebrated 40 years in that position in June 2000. The Cardinal had us in stitches as he described how Bishop McGill had been his 'guru' when he was a young student at Blairs College in Aberdeen. Then, as Father Stephen McGill, he had been Spiritual Director in the junior seminary. The Cardinal proceeded to embarrass Bishop McGill by describing him as the perfect role model for any young student for the priesthood.

In all of these visits Cardinal Winning displayed his humour and his love of being in the company of people.

An outstanding memory of each of the Cardinal's visits was his stamina and ability to stay on his feet all evening in the cathedral hall after the mass. He took time to talk to people, individually and in groups. Wearing his black suit, he always loved it when a parishioner didn't recognise him and asked: 'And what parish are you in, Father?'

He always made it so easy for me to invite him simply by his readiness to accept. He made it feel as if he was being honoured by the invitation rather than the other way around.

The Right Rev. John Mone is Bishop of Paisley.

A CELEBRATION BY

THE RIGHT REV. IAN MURRAY.

Cardinal Thomas Winning was a regular visitor to the Diocese of Argyll and the Isles, staying with priests who had been fellow students at Blairs College Aberdeen and the Scots College in Rome.

In particular, he would visit Canon Iain Gillies whom he had first met at Blairs College while studying philosophy. They frequently holidayed together and sadly it was during one such holiday in August 1983 that Canon Gillies suffered an illness and died. Cardinal Winning was very saddened by the loss.

Following the visit to Scotland by Pope John Paul II in June 1982, and in response to the Pope's invitation to all Scottish Christians to 'walk together', the Cardinal and other bishops joined Scottish church leaders in an ecumenical pilgrimage to Iona.

This was almost an 'ecumenical bridge too far' for some and it was further exacerbated by the group being so large it was necessary for most to share rooms on the island and not necessarily with someone of the same faith! At the end of the day, however, its success was a measure of the commitment to ecumenism on the part of all who were involved.

Cardinal Winning took part in an Ecumenical Triduum of Prayer in St Columba's Cathedral in Oban to mark its 1,400th anniversary in July 1997, and he was the principal concelebrant at the closing mass, at which the Nuncio, Archbishop Barbarito, assisted. It was the last public engagement of the Nuncio, and to mark his retirement the Scottish bishops presented him with a Celtic cross as a parting gift.

At my own episcopal ordination, Cardinal Winning was a co-consecrator together with Archbishop Pablo Puente and Archbishop Keith Patrick O'Brien, the principal celebrant.

The weather could hardly have been worse and the Cardinal and Nuncio had to switch from car to train because of the serious flooding on many of the roads to Oban. Everyone was worried that they might not make it. But true to fashion they arrived on time in horrendous driving rain, walking up the station platform, smiling and acting as though it were the middle of summer.

The priests and people of the Diocese of Argyll and the Isles will always remember Cardinal Thomas Winning with great affection and gratitude as someone who was a friend to them in good times and bad.

May he rest in peace.

The Right Rev. Ian Murray is Bishop of Argyll and the Isles.

Cardinal Winning at a Mass in
Sant' Andrea delle Fratte.

A CELEBRATION BY

LEN MURRAY

he life and death of each of us has its influence on others,' wrote St Paul to the Romans. Of few people could that have been more true than of Cardinal Thomas Winning. He was a man who hugely influenced public opinion in his life and a man whose death was mourned by hundreds of thousands throughout the land. He had become the most important Church leader in the country and the one to whom the media would instantly turn to get the definitive Christian view on any subject. He was a person of great charisma, of great personality and of considerable personal sanctity. But throughout it all his sense of fun and of humour always shone through.

In 1982, when Pope John Paul II visited Scotland, I had the pleasure and the honour of being Deputy Chief Steward, Scotland, for the visit. It was a visit, incidentally, which would never have taken place but for the tireless efforts of the then Archbishop Winning.

On 1 June, the visit climaxed with the Pontiff appearing at Bellahouston Park to celebrate Mass. The weather was glorious and the occasion was unforgettable for the tens of thousands who took part. At the end of the day, and after His Holiness had departed by helicopter, the Scottish hierarchy left by coach for Edinburgh.

Cardinal Gordon Gray, who was unable to attend the Bellahouston event, hosted a dinner in Edinburgh in the evening and, along with Buchan Chalmers, who was Chief Steward, and Press Officer Hugh Farmer, I accompanied the hierarchy to the function.

The day had been scorching and accordingly Archbishop Winning and the bishops made themselves comfortable on the coach loosening cassocks and collars. As we approached Edinburgh, the Archbishop asked me to help him dress and I pointed out that acting as a temporary, unpaid valet to a mere Archbishop was small beer for a man who had just shaken hands with the Pope.

Archbishop Winning thoroughly enjoyed my observations but he quickly capped it when he reminded me that 400 years before, an Archbishop had been stoned in Edinburgh. There was a distinct possibility, he said, that another Archbishop would get stoned that night in 1982!

Len Murray KHS, KSJ, JP, BL, SSC. is a retired Glasgow solicitor and after-dinner speaker.

Copy of the Freedom Scroll

MOTHERWELL DISTRICT

At Motherwell on the THIRD day of February, Nineteen Hundred and Ninety Five

Which day, the Provost and Councillors of Motherwell District being assembled, admitted and received, do hereby

ADMIT AND RECEIVE

HIS EMINENCE

THOMAS JOSEPH CARDINAL WINNING STL, DCL

AS AN

HONORARY FREEMAN OF THE DISTRICT

with all rights, privileges and immunities thereto belonging

In recognition and appreciation of his distinguished and eminent service to the Christian faith and his elevation to the high office of Cardinal of the Roman Catholic Church and as an expression of the high esteem in which he is held by the citizens of the District

John Bonomy
Chief Executive

Artist for the Freedom Scroll was Lady Avril Watson-Stewart

A CELEBRATION BY

WILLIAM WILSON

Thomas Joseph Winning, born in Glasgow Road in Craigneuk back in 1925, in time was to prove to everyone he was a one-off and it is with a great deal of pride that I can say I was part of a unique civic ceremony in 1995, which granted him a local honour that can never be matched.

Turning the clock back to the days of the old-style Motherwell and Wishaw Town Council in 1972, Thomas Winning was honoured as the only local lad to be made bishop in the Roman Catholic Church and his career then seemed to move into orbit.

In April 1974, he was elevated to Archbishop of Glasgow and 20 years on he became Scotland's third-only cardinal since the Reformation. The timing of the ceremony proved to be highly important as, at the same time, local authorities throughout Scotland were about to undergo radical changes. Districts and regions were to be streamlined and the Motherwell authority set about drawing up a list of possible candidates to be named the first ever Freeman in the 20 year lifespan of the legislative authority. Under the guidance of the leader of the ruling Labour Group, Vincent Mathieson, it was suggested that Tom Winning, who weeks earlier had assumed the title of cardinal after a lavish ceremony in Rome, should be named as the District's one and only Freeman. In February 1995 a magnificent tribute was paid to a true local hero in the Motherwell Civic Centre.

The last major function to be staged by the departing local authority was to be one of the most memorable and emotional evenings I had experienced as a long-serving member of the Lanarkshire administration. The Cardinal was totally taken aback by the packed theatre and the huge dinner in the Civic Centre. On stage with Chief Executive Ian Bonomy and myself, as Provost, he asked how he should formally thank the Council. 'How do I address you in a letter?' he asked, 'and by the way, what is your first name?'

I replied, 'Never mind the Provost routine. Everyone knows me as plain Willie!'

In time a gracious reply arrived from Motherwell's special Freeman but today I suspect it was written tongue in cheek. I still treasure to this day a cardinal writing a personal letter to me opening with: 'Dear BILLY'

Bless you Tom.

William Wilson JP, Vice-Convener Planning & Environment Committee, North Lanarkshire Council; Motherwell District Provost 1992–96.

A CELEBRATION BY

GEORGE WILKIE

As one of the two 'official' photographers privileged to record for posterity Thomas Winning's elevation to cardinal, my lasting memories will be his boundless energy and laconic humour.

As paparazzi we were more used to tracking down celebrities, so the visit to Rome was a groundbreaking experience. Our brief from his aides was to be always there, never to be noticed, but miss nothing with the camera.

The first worry was how to address him as after all we were to be companions for almost a month. Was it to be Your Grace, Eminence, Sir?

At our first meeting I addressed the problem. He thought for a moment and said 'George, how about Tom for the moment and when there is nobody around. But, the slightest hint of black, red or purple, start thinking on your feet.' For the next month it was a mixture of Eminence, Boss, Chief . . . and Tom!

His impish humour caught me out during the first official engagement. After a Sunday service in Glasgow Possil area, I suggested to him that we attempt something different for a photograph. With great enthusiasm he said: 'Let's go to Glasgow Cathedral and photograph me at the tomb of St. Mungo.' Panic broke out amongst his aides who pointed out that the number of protocols that would be broken by a visit at such short notice might upset the Cathedral's keepers and create problems. The Archbishop replied: 'Nonsense, we can disguise ourselves. Who has a scarf I can wear?' His aides were relieved that when we reached Glasgow Cathedral . . . it was closed!

Following Cardinal Winning's elevation in Rome we lined up a picture session overlooking the Tiber near Lungotevere Avenito. As my colleague was some distance away with a telephoto lens, it was my task to position him on the river-bank, as you will see on the back cover of this book. As the shots were taken I looked up into the deep blue sky where two vapour trails had appeared between Rome's two airports and formed the perfect St Andrew's Cross above the Cardinal's head.

'Do you think that could be a sign?' said I.

As quick as a flash, and I knew that he knew what I was alluding to, he said 'You're right George . . . Craig Brown is on to a winner next month!'

In the 11 days that followed he set a remarkable and punishing working pace from 7.00 a.m.

to 10.30 p.m. with regularity. During the celebrations he insisted that he met as many of the Scots who had made the journey as possible, and no one could help but be impressed by that stamina. Nothing was too much trouble for him.

A month is not a long time to get to know someone, but every minute of November 1994 was a gem.

George Wilkie is a photojournalist.

Cardinal Winning's sister, Mrs Margaret
McCarron and housekeeper 'Mrs Mac' receive
communion from Pope John Paul II.

A CELEBRATION BY

DIXON BLACKSTOCK

y meetings with the Archbishop of Glasgow Thomas Winning, later elevated to cardinal, were exclusively on the social and soccer side of life.

As a football writer for a Scottish Sunday newspaper and, for a period, the Secretary of the Scottish Football Writers' Association, we came into contact briefly at a variety of functions mainly for charitable causes in the West of Scotland.

The phrase 'man of the people' and most definitely not 'we arra people!', tends to be overused and as a result can at times be undervalued, but the phrase truly fitted this man.

Tom Winning never closeted himself behind a religious barrier and at no time did he lose touch with life. He certainly never lost his splendid sense of humour.

He chuckled when I once told him I was not a church-goer since there wasn't one between my then home in Balmoral Crescent on the south side of Glasgow and the slyly-named Queens Park Café, which sold a very pale coffee in a pint glass.

I recall taking a real chance to test his sense of humour to the full while covering a game at Parkhead during a period when the Archbishop's beloved Celtic were struggling through the season, having lost five of their last seven games, including the New Year derby against Old Firm rivals Rangers at Ibrox.

It was just five days after the Ibrox defeat and, as the Archbishop looked on, Celtic was clearly toiling against Hibs at home and the game ultimately ended in rather a tame draw. As the press box at time was close to where he was sitting I was able to attract his attention and fired off the quip: 'I don't suppose there is the slightest chance you will be changing your name to "Archbishop Losing" is there?' Tom fixed me with the kind of look that I imagined must have sent many of his junior priests into hiding! But then, after a telling silence with a stern face, he burst out laughing, shook his head and said 'Oh, Dixon, you are a terrible man!' and went on his way.

I hardly think it likely I would be mentioned in any prayers the following day.

He was formidable, but the man who became Cardinal had a wonderful sense of fun!

Dixon Blackstock is a freelance journalist and a member and past Secretary of the Scottish Football Writers' Association.

A CELEBRATION BY

FRASER ELDER

ootball was a major factor in the life of Tom Winning and our paths initially crossed in the '70s soon after I left my home town of Dundee to join the Glasgow-based media.

My arrival coincided with his appointment as Archbishop of Glasgow and with my involvement in the broadcasting world, in news and sport, our meetings became frequent at charity events and press conferences.

In time, Archbishop Winning was to become one of the central figures in Scotland as the reality of a Papal visit to the United Kingdom in 1982 became a firm fact, and in the immediate build-up to Scotland's involvement I shared my most treasured moments with him.

In May 1982, the historic visit to Britain was in grave doubt following incidents during the Pope's visit to Spain and the growing tension between Argentina and the UK over the Falkland Islands. In a concerted bid to keep the UK visit on track, a British delegation including Cardinals Hume and Gray travelled to Rome and, as no positive decision could be reached, Archbishop Winning flew to Italy to help the cause.

I was on late-night broadcasting duty and the editorial staff agreed that Tom Winning's likely dramatic intervention in Rome was a headline story of the weekend. However, I was unable to contact him until a few minutes before the news broadcast and then only by telephone. I suggested we would have to carry out a live question and answer interview.

After introducing the item I asked the Archbishop: 'The last few weeks have been nerve-racking but how do you think things will work out?'

He replied, 'Well Fraser, I think Celtic played consistently well this season and we tied up the title with a terrific win over St Mirren last week. I do think we can confidently now go for three championships in a row!'

In time the great day took place at Bellahouston and, as I stood in the press area, I swear to this day the Archbishop had a twinkle in his eye as he recalled the night fitba' was just as important as a historic Papal visit.

Fraser Elder D.A. (Scot) is a sports journalist and author.

Cardinal Winning with his young
nephews and niece.

A CELEBRATION BY

THE RIGHT REV. VINCENT LOGAN

One of my lasting and favourite memories of Cardinal Thomas Winning was his first official visit to the Diocese of Dunkeld soon after being nominated cardinal in 1994.

He came to preside at an outdoor service in the grounds of Wellburn House in Dundee and he led the service, preaching to a congregation of over 2,000 people.

Afterwards, there were refreshments at a reception in a marquee but the Cardinal neither saw nor tasted anything. He preferred to stand and greet the visitors as they went along for refreshments and stood there chatting to everyone until literally the last person had left the grounds. I found that a great witness. He gave time to every person not thinking about his own needs and at no time glancing at his watch.

There was no doubt in my mind that through his generosity and his very humanity he was the instrument of the love, patience and compassion of Christ himself. But, if anyone had ever said that to him, I'm certain he would have said: 'Och away you go!'

The fact of the matter is that through his person he did mediate Christ. In the Gospels, Christ was revealed as 'both-and' and not 'either-or'. He (Christ) was both kind and compassionate, especially to those in need, and was firm in speaking out against injustice and hypocrisy. I think Cardinal Winning showed the essential 'both-and' of Christianity and this is the reason he was so respected by Christians of all denominations.

As a colleague I always found the Cardinal great fun to be with, no matter how serious or difficult the topic. He had one of the sharpest wits I have known and I shall continue to relay witty anecdotes which I have gathered over the last 20 years as well as paying tribute to the unique contributions which he made to the Catholic Church in Scotland and to the country itself.

The Right Rev. Vincent Logan is Bishop of Dunkeld.

A CELEBRATION BY

BISHOP MARIO CONTI

A great deal has been written and said in tribute to Cardinal Tom Winning and I would wish to refer to his intellectual and spiritual springs.

As a colleague and friend he was true and there was nothing sentimental or cloying about his friendship. In personal relationships he was no different from his public persona: direct, witty and decisive. It was these qualities which sharply defined him as an exceptional person. He was intelligent and quick-witted . . . in fact the most quick-witted person I have ever known. This could be extremely funny, although if you were caught off guard you were immediately at a disadvantage. Self-defence taught you to risk the offensive! At this level his colleagues will miss him greatly as we all enjoyed his repartee.

We will also miss his leadership as he never flagged. He constantly confronted issues he considered important and he had the knack of addressing them memorably and forcefully. Even those who did not fully agree with him saw a man of integrity whose actions were as eloquent as his words.

Cardinal Tom Winning was not a profoundly philosophical man. He did not come to faith by reason, but by birth and education, which is not to suggest his response to faith was unreasoning or unreasonable. It was intelligent. He did not see Christianity as an opinion, but as a conviction that God had spoken to Christ . . . and that was it! The Church was the inheritor and guardian of that truth and his duty was to proclaim and defend it.

Cardinal Thomas Winning was a product of the pre-Vatican II Church and a convert to the post-Vatican II Church. He had all the zeal of a convert and 'reading the sign of the times' was one of his favourite catchphrases.

The results were his adoption of pastoral plans for the archdiocese which sought to establish grass-roots communication and faith-sharing cells. He may have been saddened at the leaking of the Catholic community over the years but greatly heartened by the emergence of a strong group of Catholic laity on whom so much of the future of the Church in Glasgow and throughout Scotland will depend.

There is a Latin saying: '*De mortuis nihil nisi bonum*' which means you should say nothing but what is good of those who have died. This has not been difficult in the case of Cardinal Thomas Winning.

He has bequeathed to the Church a whole set of agencies in service to the poor or, in more modern parlance, 'the disadvantaged'. In this sense he was 'the people's Cardinal' to whom we will all be indebted for many years to come. I think the underlying virtues in Cardinal Tom deserve our recognition as by such recognition we can ourselves find encouragement.

The Rt. Reverend Mario Conti is Bishop of Aberdeen.

Scots fans grasp at Cardinal Winning's
hand through the railing of the Vatican.

A CELEBRATION BY

TONY DOCHERTY

A personal celebration of my long association with Cardinal Tom Winning centres mainly on the memorable month of November 1994, when Pope John Paul II named him a cardinal priest in the title of Sant' Andrea delle Fratte in a wonderful ceremony in Rome.

With my wife Janis, I made the pilgrimage to Italy with 2,000 others from all over Scotland and, at close quarters, was able to marvel at his remarkable 'common touch' with people from all walks of life.

Initially, we met during his spell as Auxiliary Bishop at Our Holy Redeemer's church in Clydebank and, more often than not, we were both involved in funeral services in the area.

In April 1974 when he was appointed Archbishop of Glasgow in succession to Archbishop Scanlan, I was 'adopted' as his unofficial chauffeur. His firm philosophy was never to be a 'driving person' as he was aware of the dangers of being spotlighted in the event of committing a motoring offence!

One outstanding memory I have is of a telegram of congratulations my wife and I received from him soon after our wedding in Bearsden in 1975, but this was completely topped by sharing his experience in Rome some 19 years later – his deserved elevation to the position of cardinal, only the third ever in Scotland.

The measure of this man was there for all to see as hundreds of Scots poured into the Italian capital for the Vatican ceremonies and he contrived successfully to turn the whole event into a massive party for each and every one of his supporters!

As the flights arrived from Scotland late at night, the Cardinal elect was on hand to welcome and shake hands with every one of the 2,000 passengers at the Leonardo da Vinci airport.

While it was believed that priests from around 30 different countries were to be honoured, it was Tom Winning and his huge fan club that made the biggest impact! In a carnival atmosphere, the sound of the bagpipes became a regular rallying call throughout Rome and, in a simple ceremony, the Holy Father was even presented with a bottle of special whisky by the Scots contingent.

It was a never-to-be-forgotten experience and truly worthy of the man who inspired such national pride and religious passion.

Tony Docherty is the one of the leading funeral directors in Scotland.

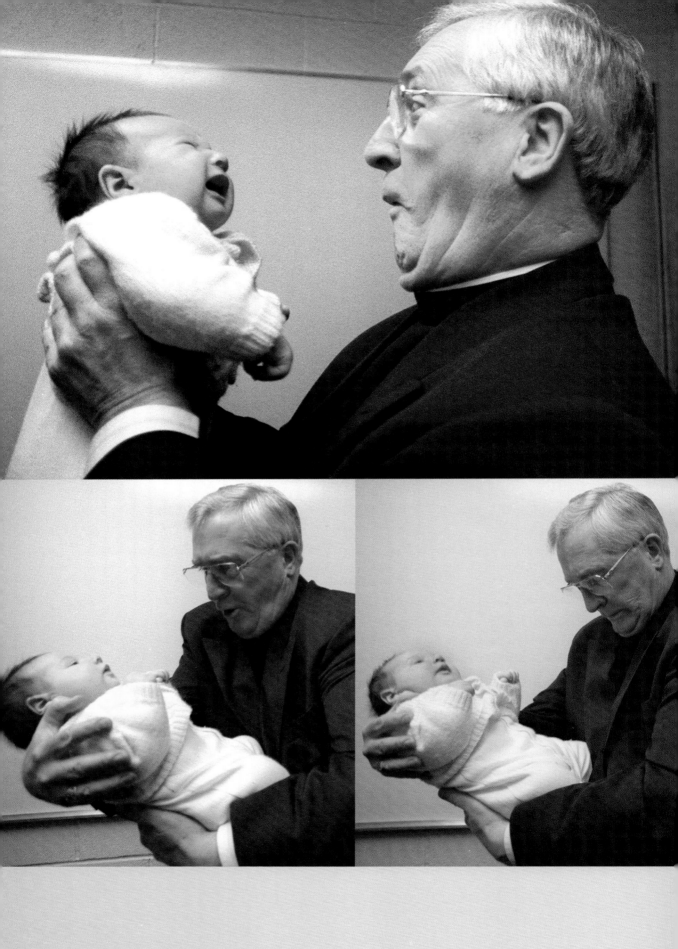

A CELEBRATION BY

HENRY McLEISH MSP

Scotland misses Thomas Winning immensely. He was a massive figure at the heart of public life in Scotland. People of all faiths respected his strong moral leadership and commitment to social justice. He was a great Scot with a real sense of pride in his country. I miss him and there is absolutely no doubt that his country misses him. He made an enormous contribution to public life; he was a towering figure and his great achievements will be remembered for many years.

I think the episode that most vividly illustrates the kind of man Tom was came when we visited Rome together to celebrate the 400th anniversary of the Scots College.

In his sermon Tom said that, for the College, the best was yet to come. Despite not always seeing eye-to-eye on some issues, I share those sentiments completely and have quoted Tom on many occasions.

I think we shared the hope that, for Scotland too, the best was yet to come.

I greatly respected his continued concern for the ordinary people of Scotland; throughout his life he strove to improve the lives of all Scots.

He was a genuine man of the people who was a great example to everyone. He was committed to social justice before the phrase was even invented. But his burning commitment to social justice did not end with Scotland – he was also a passionate opponent of poverty in the Third World.

But, above all, Tom was someone I greatly respected and admired as a person. I knew him for many years and he never changed one bit. I shared a passion for football with him, although, as he pointed out, he enjoyed marginally more success following his beloved Celtic than I ever did following East Fife! We shared countless conversations about football, although I think, above everything else, I will remember him for his down-to-earth sense of humour.

Like Donald Dewar – another great Scot who is much loved and much missed – he had a terrific wit and was the master of the one-liner.

I once hosted a reception for Tom and the Moderator of the Church of Scotland at Bute House in Edinburgh. As only he could, Tom took a look around this impressive building and laughed to me saying: 'Aye Henry, not bad for a working-class boy!'

Henry McLeish MSP is First Minister of Scotland.

137

3 June 1925
17 June 2001

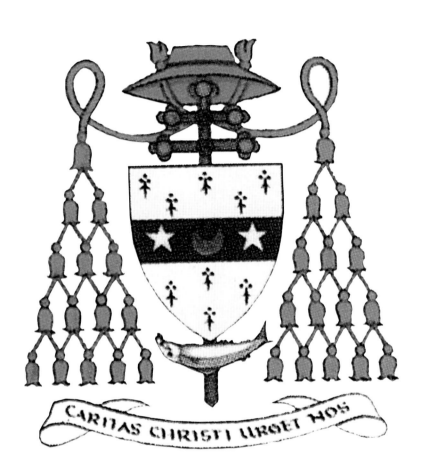

CARITAS CHRISTI URGET NOS

ACKNOWLEDGEMENTS

The authors would like to thank everyone who has taken time out from their busy schedules to contribute to the project.

Special thanks go to:
  Bishop J. Devine for his help and support
  The Dioceses of:
      Aberdeen
      Argyll & the Isles
      Dunkeld
      Galloway
      Motherwell
      Paisley
      St Andrews & Edinburgh
  Glasgow City Council
  North Lanarkshire Council
  Impact-Status
  Photonews Scotland Ltd
  The Pontifical Council of Social Communication
  Motherwell Heritage Centre
  Scottish Football League
  Len Murray for his enthusiasm and encouragement
  Russell Galbraith for his kind permission to use and research parts of his Caledonian Television video *The Winning Way*
  Doug Salteri at SMG for use of the late Arthur Kinloch pictures of the Pope at Bellahouston Park
  L'Osservatore Romano for use of elevation ceremony picture in the Vatican
  Fujifilm for their generosity and technical assistance in helping set up a complimentary photographic exhibition – especially John Cohen and John Grayston
  Father John Morrison for encyclopaedic knowledge of Rome streets and parks
  Peter MacMahon, Press Officer to Scotland's First Minister
  All the backroom team at Mainstream Publishing especially Ailsa, Jess and Becky

INDEX